2151 Old Brick Road
Glen Allen, Va 23060

Understanding the Dynamics of Typical People:
An Introduction to Jungian Type Theory

JAN 0 3 2011

About the Authors

Richard Bents, PhD, taught Educational Psychology at the University of Minnesota, and was Director of Graduate Education at Hamline University. He is partner of Future Systems Consulting. Richard Bents specializes in leadership development, personal and organizational change and transformation. He is the co-author of several books on personality and learning, and together with Reiner Blank co-author of the first German version of the MBTI.

Reiner Blank, PhD, studied theology, psychology and sociology in the USA, Switzerland and Germany. He directed a national institute for church development in Germany. Now, as partner of Future Systems Consulting GmbH, he coaches the implementation of change and transformational processes in corporations internationally. With his focus on ethics and the value added dimensions of trust in organizations, he and Richard Bents focus on the measurability of non-linear factors in organizations. He co-authored several books on change and typology.

About the Cartoonist

Werner Tiki Kustenmacher, born in 1953, is a German theologian, writer and cartoonist. He became internationally known with his book *How to Simplify Your Life*, which has been translated into 40 languages. Tiki is married to Marion; they have three children and live near Munich, Germany.

Understanding the Dynamics of Typical People:
An Introduction to Jungian Type Theory

Richard Bents
Partner, Future Systems Consulting, Inc., Saint Paul, MN

Reiner Blank
Future Systems Consulting GmbH, Hamburg, Germany

Library of Congress Cataloging in Publication
is available via the Library of Congress Marc Database under the
LC Control Number 2010922293

Library and Archives Canada Cataloguing in Publication

Bents, Richard H.
 Understanding the dynamics of typical people : an introduction
to Jungian type theory / Richard Bents, Reiner Blank.

Translation of: Typisch Mensch.
Includes bibliographical references.
ISBN 978-0-88937-382-2

 1. Myers-Briggs Type Indicator. 2. Typology (Psychology).
I. Blank, Reiner, 1948- II. Title.

BF698.8.M94B4613 2010   155.2'64   C2010-901186-4

All cartoons © 1995 Werner Tiki Küstenmacher

© 2010 by Hogrefe Publishing

PUBLISHING OFFICES
USA: Hogrefe Publishing, 875 Massachusetts Avenue, 7th Floor,
 Cambridge, MA 02139
 Phone (866) 823-4726, Fax (617) 354-6875;
 E-mail customerservice@hogrefe-publishing.com
EUROPE: Hogrefe Publishing, Rohnsweg 25, 37085 Göttingen, Germany
 Phone +49 551 49609-0, Fax +49 551 49609-88,
 E-mail publishing@hogrefe.com

SALES & DISTRIBUTION
USA: Hogrefe Publishing, Customer Services Department,
 30 Amberwood Parkway, Ashland, OH 44805
 Phone (800) 228-3749, Fax (419) 281-6883,
 E-mail customerservice@hogrefe.com
EUROPE: Hogrefe Publishing, Rohnsweg 25, 37085 Göttingen, Germany
 Phone +49 551 49609-0, Fax +49 551 49609-88,
 E-mail publishing@hogrefe.com

OTHER OFFICES
CANADA: Hogrefe Publishing, 660 Eglinton Ave. East, Suite 119-514, Toronto,
 Ontario, M4G 2K2
SWITZERLAND: Hogrefe Publishing, Länggass-Strasse 76, CH-3000 Bern 9

Hogrefe Publishing
Incorporated and registered in the Commonwealth of Massachusetts, USA, and in Göttingen,
Lower Saxony, Germany

No part of this book may be reproduced, stored in a retrieval system or transmitted, in any
form or by any means, electronic, mechanical, photocopying, microfilming, recording or
otherwise, without written permission from the publisher.

Printed and bound in the USA
ISBN: 978-0-88937-382-2

Table of Contents

1 Introduction 1
1.1 Human Typology 1
1.2 "Typical..." 2
1.3 What This Book Is All About 4
1.4 Bridging the Gap – From Empirical Observations to Typology 5

2 Beginnings 7

3 Type Theory 10
3.1 Introduction to Type Theory 10
3.2 Typical Objections to Type 11
3.3 Assumptions of Type Theory 12
3.4 Determining Type 13
3.5 The Four Basic Scales 14

4 Basic Functions and Attitudes 16
4.1 Perceiving Functions: Sensing and Intuition 16
4.2 Judging Functions: Thinking and Feeling 23
4.3 Attitude Toward Outer or Inner World: Extraversion (E) and Introversion (I) 28
4.4 Lifestyle (Attitude Toward Outside World): Judging and Perceiving 33
4.5 Validation 37

5 Type Dynamics 38
5.1 Dominant Function for Extraverted Types (E) 40
5.2 Dominant Function for Introverted Types (I) 41
5.3 Tertiary and Inferior Function 41
5.4 Summary – Dynamics of Type 42

6 Description of the Individual Types 45
6.1 Short Descriptions 46
6.2 Description of the 16 Types 48
    ENFP – Extraverted/iNtuitive/Feeling/Perceiving 49
    ENFJ – Extraverted/iNtuitive/Feeling/Judging 52
    ENTP – Extraverted/iNtuitive/Thinking/Perceiving 55
    ENTJ – Extraverted/iNtuitive/Thinking/Judging 58
    ESFP – Extraverted/Sensing/Feeling/Perceiving 61
    ESFJ – Extraverted/Sensing/Feeling/Judging 64
    ESTP   Extraverted/Sensing/Thinking/Perceiving 67

	ESTJ	–	Extraverted/Sensing/Thinking/Judging	70
	INFP	–	Introverted/iNtuitive/Feeling/Perceiving	73
	INFJ	–	Introverted/iNtuitive/Feeling/Judging	76
	INTP	–	Introverted/iNtuitive/Thinking/Perceiving	78
	INTJ	–	Introverted/iNtuitive/Thinking/Judging	81
	ISFP	–	Introverted/Sensing/Feeling/Perceiving	84
	ISFJ	–	Introverted/Sensing/Feeling/Judging	87
	ISTP	–	Introverted/Sensing/Thinking/Perceiving	90
	ISTJ	–	Introverted/Sensing/Thinking/Judging	93

7 Stress ... 96
7.1 Definition of Stress ... 97
7.2 Controlled Stress ... 98
7.3 Uncontrolled Stress ... 99
7.4 Summary ... 100
7.5 Stress by Type ... 101

8 Practical Application ... 117
8.1 Leadership ... 117
8.2 Communication ... 122
8.3 Learning ... 126
8.4 Teamwork ... 128

9 Summary ... 131

10 References ... 132

1 Introduction

John Pritchard looked across that gorgeous valley. He smiled. Had his friend Mike come with him to this favorite place, Mike would have talked and talked and talked – gliding through the clouds with his imaginary plane, creating one vision after the other, expressing passionate views and visions combined with fairy tales. John instead remained quietly focused on the precipice 5 miles ahead, calculated his approach time, and mentally rechecked his gear: cams, nuts, bolts, pitons, rope, binder, bird beak, chalk. He carried only what he needed – not more. He wanted to leave no booty.

People are different, indeed. John and Mike were friends, but seemingly opposite patterns of personality challenged and at the same time solidified their relationship. John remembered – he would have written Mike off some 12 years ago, when they first met. However, they were linked by position and function in their company and they were thrust together to solve a highly complex and knotty political problem. In those first meetings, it was like they were talking different languages and oh so frustrating. If they had not gotten their act together, the project would have failed in the first weeks. A miracle happened. Trust grew within and between. Appreciation was expressed, and they succeeded – together – their two worlds merged without John or Mike losing their own unique identity.

1.1 Human Typology

Understanding and appreciating another's unique identity is not always easy. Fortunately, we have tools, supports, and models to assist us. Typology is one such model. Being anything other than pigeonholing people, typology, or *typing*, is an intelligent radar system and organizing strategy. It provides structure for the mind that not only enables us to remain sane, but also illustrates commonalities, draws distinctions, and creates higher levels of conscious awareness. A typology allows us to be:

- Conscious of those trained patterns within our own psyche;
- Able to navigate foggy landscapes when stressed;
- Appreciative of differences between and among people; and
- Aware of the synergies between people who are different (like John and Mike).

Theory of psychological type, as articulated by Carl Gustav Jung,[1] is our typology of choice. It is highly theoretical, exceedingly practical, and widely applied. We will refer to several different surveys and indicators that are based on Jung's psychological type as they attempt to type people. Our primary focus is to make typing practical, regardless of the tool or approach that may be used. In our suggested application of the results of these surveys and indicators, we will attempt to remain as true to Jung as we can. No theory has been as well-marketed, well-researched, popularly utilized, or as well-accepted as Jung's theory of psychological type.

Typing is practical. When you know your type, you begin to appreciate and access complex interdependencies within a person, team, or organization. You know that if a team member fails to interact, or if people do not cooperate during a change process, then it's more than gravel in the gearbox. Frictions and blockades lead to energy loss and minimization of the return on investment. Many mergers and acquisitions fail because people and corporate cultures don't synchronize. Coming from different places, viewing the world differently, and exercising different approaches to making decisions often create challenges. It is these people issues that create most of the difficulties. Typing takes people and culture into consideration. Actually, people and corporate cultures are primary to success in most ventures and therefore opportunities to reduce friction and blockades ought to be understood and implemented. This understanding energizes the workforce, unites people and cultures, and creates higher return on investment.

We invite you to learn the practical use of type theory. Remember, according to Albert Einstein, a theory is only as good as it offers practical insight into realities.

1.2 "Typical..."

Mr. Bates prefers accuracy. Each morning he is at his desk at 8:15 a.m. – on time. His colleague, Mrs. Nelson, is a few minutes late – again. She senses a critical glance even though Mr. Bates does not look up. She can see his profile and notices his short glance and barely a nod. She is annoyed. He seems to look for mistakes and shortcomings and always finds something. This morning she met her boss in the elevator and she requested reassignment to another department.

Consider Mrs. Sims. People around her know she focuses on her tasks. She likes to have problems clearly defined; details and facts are important to her. The first impression she leaves with her colleagues is distant, aloof, and analytic. Jamie Jones, her coworker next door, finds that Mrs. Sims' fanaticism for routine would rob his energy completely. He loves to work on several things at the same time. And, unlike Mrs. Sims, he looks forward to that coffee break, because then he meets his colleagues from the other departments and can catch up on all the latest news. He loves the atmosphere of togetherness. If the atmosphere is dead, then this is the beginning of the end – and thus Jamie.

1 Introduction

Mrs. Sims, of course, could tell Jamie many stories involving proven disastrous financial loss because someone overlooked the details and the facts. By the way, she considers the "good spirit" next door superficial and does not like his stroll over to the coffee pot – coffee breaks take too long, colleagues talk all the time when they are supposed to work, and so on. She cannot imagine that her push for clarity and structure could trigger anger or anxieties with Jamie. These stories go on and on every day in life at the workplace. We can all sing quite a few verses of this song.

Psychology of everyday life merely needs a contoured characteristic to create an opinion in the environment of being a "typical pedant" or being "superficial." Thoughtless and unreflecting, we speak of the *typical* scholar, or the *typical* public officer – not to mention the *typical* Englishman or whatever nationality. Such generalities are unqualified and not very helpful. They tend to put people in boxes and do not improve communication, cooperation, or living together. In this book we speak about types, yes – but in a different and more qualified way. We speak about type dynamics within the person and within communities.

Assumption: People can be typed. This happens every day, obviously. We cannot help but look for patterns, categories, typical behaviors, and personality traits. Neurobiologists would say that's how our brain functions – period.

We know each person has certain preferences that influence behaviors in everyday life. A key question for us is: How can people employ their notions in such a productive way that they better build and cultivate relationships with other people so that good cooperation is possible?

We hope and expect, as you read this book critically and intently, that you will sharpen your awareness of your own typical behaviors. If you abide by Plato's advice of *gnoti se-auton* (know yourself), you automatically sharpen your sensitivity for your preferences and for the preferences of others in your environment as well.

Each of us has nurtured specific attitudes and preferences in the course of life. Healthy development of the psyche depends on how one cultivates and differentiates preferences. By being consciously aware and appreciative of differences between and among people, knowing one's own preferences, and recognizing, respecting, and integrating those perceptions in our own behaviors, we will get along much better in both personal and professional workspace.

Men and women can contribute to a constructive, positive, and caring community. Deeper understanding of different types and of people with their characteristic profile could be a productive service of psychology for our societies.

As mentioned, the typing and categorization of people takes place constantly and everywhere. At a birthday party, the woman in the green dress might remind you of a good friend or your mother. The typing begins as certain linings create the image of a type. Your mother, being punctual and proper, prefers prior arrangements and clear deadlines and, so too, perhaps does the woman in the green dress.

However, for another person (in the red dress), this is like a corset that is too tight; she wants to be free, flexible, and celebrate the exotic chaos that always seems to surround her. Now, as you approach the woman in the red dress (or the woman in the green dress, according to your preference), you have already preconceived ideas about her. But how substantiated are your ideas? If your ideas are not reasonably valid, you could be in for some uncomfortable surprises or tense moments – perhaps embarrassingly so.

Embarrassing moments happen when ideas are not valid. Tensions grow when different people like Mrs. Sims and Jamie Jones are forced together in the same office and expected to work together, but they do not hold accurate perceptions of each other. Why? One reason is because each one has different preferences and they lack awareness on the part of the other of what these preferences might be and how they are exhibited in behavior. We act according to our own preferences, and we see others through our own rose-colored glasses.

Behaviors provoke positive or negative tensions between people who are different. Take, for example, the couple planning their long-desired vacation together: *She* dreams of that secluded island where she finally can sit down and read and reflect, let her thoughts wander, and discover the inner worlds again. For *him*, the lonely island triggers horror scenarios; he needs others, he wants to party and be connected with many people in addition to his internet and cell phone connections. How will this vacation turn out?

1.3 What This Book Is All About

Our intention is to help you recognize and differentiate personality types and profiles so that you may explore whether or not these perspectives of people can help you understand and deal with complex realities.

This book should help you to self-assess. It ought to create a conscious awareness of how you perceive the world and how you make decisions. You will not find quick answers or easy recipes. You will find direction. It may take some focused reflection and/or open discussion, but you will become more self-aware. On the solid ground of type theory, we offer access and support to unlock complex personality constructs. These approaches are proven, tried, and applicable in many different contexts. Please follow step by step – even if it might seem somewhat theoretical at times. And enjoy. Enjoy the process of self discovery and the dynamics of how you (and others) function.

One of the basic assumptions of psychology is that psychologically healthy people hold an accurate self-assessment, positive self-acceptance, and high self-esteem. For health's sake and an ability to better assess others, you ought to know yourself first. We endeavor to provide you with ample opportunity to reflect your self. Typing is an out-of-the-box perspective on the basis of certain "objective" parameters and a beginning understanding of the dynamics of personality. Some of your reflective thoughts (or discussions with others) may take you out of the box. That's good. You ought not be pigeonholed.

Identity is key. Therefore, keep searching for who you are. Do not trust any simple "three rules of how to be successful and get your life out of the rut" programs. Be diligent. Appreciate your personal strengths and never lose the respect and wonder for that unique individuality of each person. Typology, when understood and used with integrity, can help to identify the individuality and the authenticity of each person. Finding self is a central first step in this human quest.

We invite you to take a walk with us. Many methods have been developed over time to help understand self and others. The approaches are all meant to serve as maps, guidelines, and parameters for the quest of finding self. In addition to self-discovery, typing can be and is used in leadership training, team building, and career counselling in social institutions and many companies. We offer a time-tested map (the application of Jung's theory). You are the critical authority and you will make the final decisions as to whether or not it is the right direction for you. Of course, we suggest that the most effective route would be to discuss your type with an expert coach. The second best route is an intelligent display – an authentic process that causes you to reflect and think. That is the offer with this book.

1.4 Bridging the Gap – From Empirical Observations to Typology

Typing is based on empirical observation. Typology naturally emerges when one observes nature and humanity. The ancients first explored typologies as they tried to explain human behavior. Ancient Greek physician Hippocrates (460–377 CE) correlated four human temperaments with the four elements – air, water, fire, and earth – based on different mixes of body fluids. Two hundred years later, the Roman medic Galenus assigned this idea to four types that we still refer to today: *sanguine*, *phlegmatic*, *choleric*, and *melancholic*. Galenus popularized those types. No question, the world view of those type fathers is antique for us moderns, so let's move to a context that is a bit more familiar to us.

Prominent type scholar Ernst Kretschmar based his research on "Physique and Character."[2] His intention was to connect the physical constitution of people with psychic structure (personality). Kretschmar's system is voluminous and multidimensional. In his introduction, he quoted a popular notion that caricatures (types) temperament and outward appearance:

In the mind of the man-in-the-street, the devil is usually lean and has a thin beard growing on a narrow chin, while the fat devil has a strain of good-natured stupidity. The intriguer has a hunch-back and a slight cough. The old witch shows us a withered hawk-like face. Where there is brightness and jollity we see the fat knight Falstaff – red-nosed and with shining pate. The peasant woman with a sound knowledge of human nature is undersized, tubby, and stands with her arms akimbo. Saints look abnormally lanky, long-limbed, of penetrating vision, pale, and godly. To put it shortly; the virtuous and the devil must have a pointed nose, while the comic must have a fat one. What are we to say to all this? At first only this much: It may be that phenomena, which the fantasy of the people has crystallized into the tradition of centuries, are objective documents of folk-psychology – jotting from the observation of mankind, worthy, perhaps, of a glance even from the eyes of the experimenter.[2]

This humoresque introduction to "Physique and Character" captures empirical studies over many years that correlated people's bodily appearance and typical personality traits. As with all typologies, Kretschmar describes in paper version his type theory in the purest of forms: The condensed forms of individual characteristics. The scholar also calculates those blurred mixed forms of type. But tendencies of type descriptions in this or the other direction are obvious and somewhat verifiable.

We conclude with Kretschmar: On the basis of empirical evidence a certain physique can be traced. Types can be indexed. Kretschmar extended his observations and included typical behaviors and personality traits. On the basis of empirical studies, he established a relationship between body structure and psychic characteristics.

This is not the place to delve into details of his physiotypes or certain characteristics. But we point out the generic procedure: *Observing behavioral patterns and specified physical traits can lead to hypotheses of differentiated psychological types.*

In this context, we focus on psychic processes as researched and described by the Swiss physician and psychoanalyst Carl Gustav Jung. For many years, Jung studied how people function. Dealing with patients of all social strata and "from the critical point of my own psychological idiosyncrasies," he published his book *Psychological Types* in 1921 (English edition, 1923). Jung wanted the intelligent layperson be able to reflect this "conscious psychology," as noted in the preface of his book. Katherine Briggs and her daughter, Isabel Briggs-Myers, were inspired by Jung's assumptions and descriptions and worked for over 30 years to construct a practical instrument: The Myers–Briggs Type Indicator (MBTI),[3] which had as a primary objective to make Jung's theory of personality type practical and available to as many people as possible. The MBTI has been the most popular "type tool" to date. John Golden's Personality Type Profiler (GPTP),[4] which gives a differentiated analysis of type, is another highly popular example of type surveys. Other instruments designed to identify Jungian psychological types exist as well, including the Jungian Type Survey (Grey–Wheelwrights Tests, GWT),[5] the Singer–Loomis Type Deployment Inventory (SL-TDI),[6] and the Jungian Type Index (JTI),[7] all of which are widely used. We encourage the use of psychological types. The method used to determine type is less important as long as the tool is reliable and valid.

2 Beginnings

Is there really anything like a normative understanding of human behavior? Our socialized postmodern sense of freedom and individuality shies away from that kind of notion, of course. And it is good to remember that, for Jung, the conception of *normative behavior* was no antinomy for a conviction that every human being is unique and distinctive. Each person is unique and distinctive, yet patterns exist.

Unique yet common, typical: That was Jung's basic proposition for his concept of individuation (the life-long process of becoming self). The journey of becoming self, or working toward "completion," according to Jung, is guided by *functions* – preferences in how we perceive the world and how we make decisions. Knowing someone's function preferences enables you to understand personality development and to predict how a person will behave – assuming that they are acting consistently with their preferred functions. These function preferences are the fundamentals for Jung's type theory. His basic formula reads: Each person has a preferred way of *perceiving* and *decision making*. Jung called these psychic processes, which are common to all humans, *psychological functions*.

A person perceives (takes in information) either through *sensing* or *intuition*. A person makes decisions either on the basis of objective analysis (*thinking*) or on the basis of personal subjective value categories (*feeling*). These two dichotomous pairs of cognitive functions – the "irrational" (perceiving) functions of sensing and intuition and the "rational" (judging) functions of thinking and feeling – are the foundation of personality.

The two core functions (perceiving and judging) with their respective aspects lead to four basic patterns:

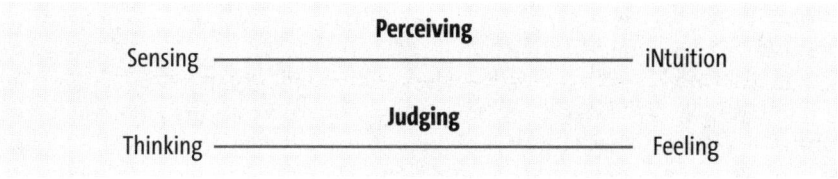

Jung continued by suggesting that we all have a source of psychic energy that is expressed as the *attitude* with which one experiences the world. Either you have (a) a preference for the outer world of fellow human beings and things (for this Jung coined the term *extraversion*); or (b) you prefer the inner world of ideas and thoughts which is consequently an *introverted* attitude. Now we map three scales:

1. A scale of psychic energy   Extraverted or Introverted
2. A scale of perception   Sensing or iNtuition
3. A scale of judging   Thinking or Feeling

Combining the attitudes with each of the four functions of perceiving and judging, we now arrive at eight personality types diagrammed as follows:

Energy
Extraversion ————————————————— Introversion

Perceiving
Sensing ————————————————— iNtuition

Judging
Thinking ————————————————— Feeling

Note: Eight different types are identified because each of the perceiving and judging functions can act in an introverted or extraverted attitude. That means the sensing perception can either be positioned extraverted (1) or introverted (2); the intuitive perception can be external (3) or internal (4); the analytical (thinking) way to make decisions can focus extraverted (5) or introverted (6); the same is true for value-based decision making (feeling) – it can be introverted (7) or extraverted (8). Remember, Jung identified 16 personality types, so there are still more to come.

The psychic processes (functions = sensing, intuition, thinking, feeling) are not static; they interact dynamically. And depending how conscious a person is of these preferences, they become more integral to our personality with time and maturity.

Within these dynamics, a *dominant* function crystallizes early in life. If we can identify the dominant function, we better understand the complex dynamics of personality and how the other functions interact. Jung was able to identify the dominant function through psychoanalysis. This took a bit of time and could only be done responsibly by trained analysts. Katherine Briggs and Isabel Briggs-Myers carefully studied Jung and the dynamics of the functions. They realized that the dominant function could be identified through careful observation of lifestyle preferences. They were able to phrase questions that would reflect particular preferences for a structured lifestyle or a more open lifestyle. Briggs and Briggs-Myers then added a fourth scale, which describes this *attitude* toward the perceiving and judging functions. On that basis, they could claim to easily identify the dominant and the secondary functions. This provides a highly practical approach to Jung's complex theory of personality type. Now, all 16 of Jung's theoretical personality types could be readily identified.

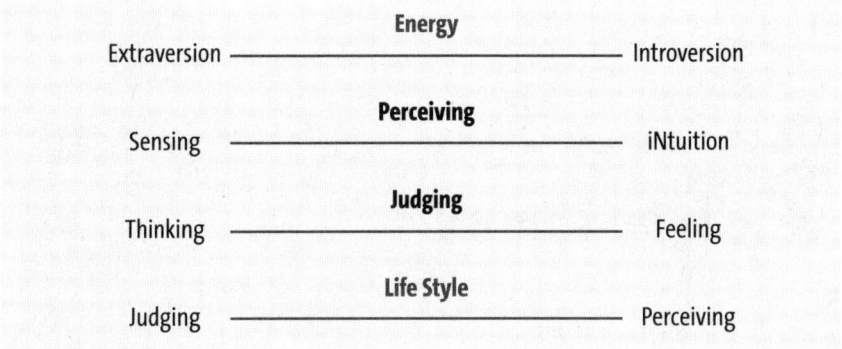

Four scales offer a combination of 16 types. All Jung's notions of the core functions of personality (perceiving and judging), the attitudes of energy and lifestyle, as well as the identification of the dominant function could all be accessed and used to understand preferences and natural personality growth.

Years of refinement of the tools used to identify personality type have yielded not only higher quality assessments, but also helpful contributions to the practical use of type. During the late 1900s, research on stress and the impact that stress has on personality led Ed and John Golden to add yet another scale to Jung's typology. The stress scale does not change Jungian theory, but demonstrates additional practical application of the theory.

Golden's Personality Type Profiler (GPTP) added a fifth scale which reports how a person reacts to stress. Of course, each person reacts differently to stress, congruent to type preferences. According to Golden, type preferences and the stress scale indicate how a person can recognize stress patterns and identify tactics to purposefully manage eustress and distress.

It is likely that there will be continued additions in the future. The Jungian basics remain, however. We look forward to continued differentiation and more ways to make the theory practical.

We now turn our attention to understanding type theory in a practical and comprehensible way. We share how you can type yourself and find out about preferences. And in the final chapters of this book we offer concrete applications for work life and everyday stress situations.

This book ends where we all want to start. Maybe you want to start reading the last part first. That is fine. However, at this point we offer a bit more basic knowledge and background information. As soon as you understand the system and the theory, practicality is obvious.

3 Type Theory

- Do you want fair treatment?
- Do you need praise and acknowledgment on a regular basis?
- Are you frustrated by insensitive responses?
- Are you irritated when someone does not put all of the facts on the table?
- Do you prefer a structured lifestyle with a results orientation?
- Would you like to know why you have answered the questions the way you did?

Type theory can help. Each person has their own amenities, biases, and predilections. Within our ingrown multiplicities, however, we find certain commonalities. With some people we communicate quite well, whereas worlds seem to separate us from others.

3.1 Introduction to Type Theory

With psychological type we use a four-letter code to identify and talk about preferences. It is self-understood that such four-letter designations do not consider the uniqueness of each person appropriately. But it is a first important step to get to know self and others better – and it leads to *conscious* appreciation of your own uniqueness. Everyday life is where we then consciously employ our characteristics when we interact with others. We experience that each person has their own way of approaching the world.

Distinguishing features of people are obvious: Starting with different imaginations, tastes, procedures, and habits to enjoy life. We are continuously confronted with the diverse way of how other people perceive the world and make decisions. Jung suggests that the seemingly inapprehensible ways of the behavioral otherness are regulated and consistent in itself. Jung contended that, while holding our individual uniqueness, each of us is more like one particular psychological type than any of the other types.

Instruments for type theory, like the MBTI, GTPT, GWT, and SL-DTI, first confirm the basic preference of the person – how he/she perceives and makes decisions. Second, the instruments make attempts to identify particular facets that mark special characteristics of the individual. Third, there is always an attempt to point to the practical impact and benefit in different areas – like relationships, workplace, career planning, or teaching and learning.

Recall Mr. Bates and Mrs. Nelson, whom we got to know at the beginning of this book. They could have created excellent synergies if they understood their different personalities in the light of type theory. They would have realized how they differed from each other. They could have learned the strengths of each other. They might have even gained greater appreciation of the other and seen how useful the perception of the other person could be for certain tasks and how the other person's preference could be an excellent precondition for a very different task.

Had Mr. Bates and Mrs. Nelson been introduced to type theory, they could have learned much about themselves and about each other. They could have exercised their new-found knowledge to solve more complex issues and attend more effectively to specific tasks. A reliable and valid approach to type theory mediates a quick and solid access to these challenges, especially when confronted with more complex realities.

However, even if Mr. Bates and Mrs. Nelson had been introduced to type theory they may have still resisted its application. As we all have natural preferences, we all have natural resistance to things as well.

3.2 Typical Objections to Type

We have already pointed out that typology is dynamic and incorporates the complex uniqueness of the individual. To use typology to pigeonhole people is unprofessional and primitive.

Interestingly, arguments against typing are also "typical" for particular types: A person with a preference for extraversion might say; "I am too busy with other things, and I don't have time to fill out a questionnaire. Can someone just ask me the questions and we can talk it over?" A person with a preference for introversion has a high sense of privacy that ought to be protected (from the introverted perspective). The introvert does not want to be exposed like that and may not be happy about disclosing their personality type.

The sensing types prefer something more concrete, fact-based, and touchable. They frown at the abstract theoretical discussion, and if results are not applicable right away, they lose interest: "Just the facts please, and show me how I can use them immediately." The iNtuitive types, though, imagine all of the possibilities that can be derived from type. They may even see books like this as a bit too simplified, too linear, and constructed. Those categories of 16 types appear too restrictive. "Why only 16 types?" they ask. They are more interested when we refer to uniqueness and x-possible types, when all of the dynamics are considered.

Thinking types often question the "soft" science of psychology. If they get past that, they are more interested in the theory and assumptions upon which typing is formulated. They appreciate the scientific rigor of the reliability and validity testing. They ask: "Does the questionnaire really offer what the theory promises?" They demand rational proof before they accept the concept. Feeling types, on the other hand, may disapprove because a system like this seems to deny the individuality and uniqueness of the person. And, of course, they distance themselves from anything that could potentially hurt people. Feeling types need to see the human benefits of type before they fully accept it.

People with a judging attitude have reservations: "I have an effective method already; show me how this method could be better." On the other side, people with a preference for perceiving like to keep things open. They don't want to commit themselves to forced-choice questionnaires and they distance themselves because being put into a category is too self-contained and final.

Many arguments could be raised against such a typing method. Pros and cons can be listed. Advantages will be obvious when we start getting into content and concrete descriptors. Some of you noted these specifics already. Some of you will need someone with whom to discuss these ideas. Others need more data and theory. We understand that; please take what you need (prefer).

On the next pages we get more into the four dimensions and specific characteristics. We describe how we move from the general dimensions to more explicit type descriptions. Finally, we offer, by way of example, how type theory can be applied to leadership, communication, learning, teamwork, and elsewhere.

3.3 Assumptions of Type Theory

Type theory, based on observations of human behavior, holds a set of assumptions. It is helpful to understand and accept these assumptions. They provide understanding and offer guidance in interpreting type:

- *Patterns exist in human behavior. It is not accidental.* Even if behavior of a person appears random, there are patterns that can be identified.
- *Therefore, human behavior is classifiable – it can be typed.* Psychological types describe patterns of how a person prefers to take in information and then structures these perceptions in coming to conclusions. Type theory assumes that each psychic activity can be clustered into four processes: two perceiving processes (via senses and intuition) and two structuring processes (analytical and value-based decision making).
- Patterning and repeated patterns of behaviors result in *preferences*. As we create conscious and subconscious patterns for ourselves and for our own orientation, we develop certain preferences. Others have different preferences.
- Preferences relate to *basic functions of our personality* that we practice life-long. Research has shown that these preferences are stable and consistent over life. Pronounced preferences or the marked degree of them might change, but tendencies are consistent over time.

- *Preferences are developed early in life* and are rudimentary for our personality. It's an academic discussion as to whether or not people are born with certain preferences. And, of course, environment may support or impede preferences. In any case, the preferences are established early.
- When certain vital issues emerge for a person, they are first communicated via the basic preferences. *Preferences "dictate"* how we experience the world and how we make decisions. Two people can react to the same stimulus quite differently.
- Preferences play an important role in determining if a person, a task, or an event is attractive or not. We can be typed. That means our *personality type can tell us in advance* what would satisfy and stimulate us, and at the same time predict what would probably irritate or frustrate us.

Furthermore, type theory is founded on basic notions of dichotomy, polar opposites, and dynamic balance. Psyche is patted in dichotomy and oppositeness. Perception via sensing and intuition are opposites. In like manner, the objective analytical thinking and subjective, value-based, feeling, decision-making processes are bipolar. The lack of understanding these dichotomous processes plays a key role in everyday controversies and conflicts.

Example: Mr Bates has a conscious preference to perceive with his senses. He has practiced and differentiated this process over time and built certain abilities around this cornerstone of his personality; he relies on it. Given that Mr. Bates has focused his attention on sensing, his intuitive perception is not as developed and he will not rely on intuitions as much as on his senses. It may result in an understandable tendency to downgrade the other side. Psychological oppositeness often becomes a battleground in the outer world.

Obviously, there is reason here. Everyday experience illustrates this basic constitution. If you concentrate on your five senses, you cannot perceive intuitively at the same time – and vice versa. Of course, you can switch to the other side of the scale. But, by definition, you cannot use both at the same time. So the preference that gets the attention gets developed, is used for differentiation, and is found interesting – all at the cost of the other side.

We experience psychic energy not just within the tension of opposites. Personality pursues a dynamic balance at the same time. That means preferences do not operate against each other, but strive for coordination. As we mature in the course of life, the nonpreferred notions demand our attention. We discuss these dynamics in Chapter 5, when we talk about the order of preferences.

3.4 Determining Type

To discern and validate one's type is worthwhile and highly valuable. For some, it's fun and easy and the result makes sense right away. For others, the process is more tedious and complicated. Some people have a clear understanding of how they function and can articulate their preferences right away and connect those insights to different dimensions of personality type. Others need assistance and look for more distinct features to analyze their preferences. Some desire an objective, analytical, and empirical procedure, whereas others prefer a more subjective, holistic, and introspective method. The method you select will be largely based on your preferences, and for all who explore their type, we recommend you validate your results. In any case, the result of determining and validiting your personality type is enriching and helpful.

The objective for self-assessing type is to identify four basic preferences on the four scales: EI, SN, TF, and JP. The scales are bipolar, with one letter on each end of the scale. The scales define the preferred functions and attitudes. We point out that typing cannot capture the behavior, quality characteristics, or ability of a person. Psychological type measures preferences of psychological energy and the choice made between two alternatives. Perhaps an analogy is useful here:

When you reach across the table for a pen, or when you try to catch a ball, you generally do it with your preferred hand. You do not think about it, you just grab instinctively. There is no conscious decision and no debate – just reaction. The same is true with personality preferences. One acts on preferred functions.

Personality preferences are not as obvious as right or left handedness, however. They are, in fact, much more complex. To identify preferences precisely, you have to observe, look closely, understand what you are seeing, and then "type" the observation. Because it is more difficult than cursory observation, we take the time now to provide sufficient explanation so that you may identify and validate your type.

If you spend extended time with type theory, your competence will increase. You will be able to recognize patterns in your own behavior as well as in the behavior of others. Observation and reflection are key. As you read the following pages, reflect on your behaviors and be sensitive to tendencies that may lean in one direction more than in the opposite direction.

You may want to repeat the observation and reflection process to check and doublecheck your own notions. Share your observations and reflections with friends and colleagues. Search for source materials or attend a workshop on type with a professional and licensed trainer. A statistically reliable and validated instrument gives you a more precise starting point. You fill out a questionnaire and get a type that usually is quite accurate. But also remember: Even the results of a good assessment are merely a set of hypotheses for you to validate or repudiate.

3.5 The Four Basic Scales

A quick review: Type is based on four bipolar scales. Two scales refer to attitudes and two scales refer to functions.

		Energy	
Attitude	Extraversion	———————	Introversion
		Perceiving	
	Sensing	———————	iNtuition
Functions		**Judging**	
	Thinking	———————	Feeling
		Life Style	
Attitude	Judging	———————	Perceiving

The possible combination of preferences yields 16 personality types.

Each pole of a scale stands in tension with its opposite. For psychic health, a dynamic balance is important. Healthy development takes place when you cultivate your preferences and use them in appropriate tension with the opposite, without pushing yourself to change them.

We continue our discussion and describe the basic dimensions. You will note that we are using the international type codes, which are used by many of the Jungian type indicators.

4 Basic Functions and Attitudes

We start with the basic functions: Perception (sensing and iNtuition) and judging (thinking and feeling). These are the middle two letters in your four-letter code. The functions are the core of your personality.

As you go through these next pages, reflect where you stand. Are you more often on the right side of each scale or more times on the left side? The scales are always structured in the same way, so try to discover your leanings – your preferences. This is a good place to continue your self-reflection. You may even want to take notes.

4.1 Perceiving Functions: Sensing and Intuition

What is your preference for perceiving the world? How do you take in information? Two people are standing near the edge of a bunch of trees. One sees the trees, the other sees the forest. They are looking at the same thing, but for the person on the right it is quickly clear: There is a forest! The person on the left looks and sees trees, different trees, perhaps focusing on just one or two, noticing the specific shade of green needles, the rough bark, and the dry needles and sparse thin grass on the ground.

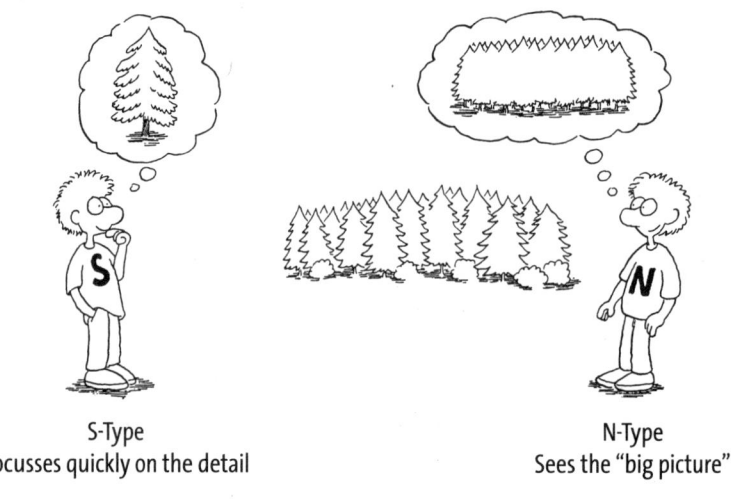

S-Type
Focusses quickly on the detail

N-Type
Sees the "big picture"

4 Basic Functions and Attitudes   17

Both are exercising sensing and intuitive perception. But the one on the left (S) prefers sensing for years and focuses first on concrete details. Reality is what you can see, touch, taste, smell, and/or hear. The sensor prefers the concrete and the practical, wants facts, trusts facts, and remembers facts. Hands-on experience is real. Present and past are the relevant time dimensions.

The one on the right – intuitive (N) – looks for the connectedness of the parts right away. The overview is the starting point – then you might talk about details, if at all. Scanning, glancing, and viewing complex ideas as complete wholes are most interesting. Hunches have proven true in the past. Those with a preference for intuition explore beyond the present. Future options are interesting and intriguing.

A few examples:

Eric was used to flying. But he would never forget that terrible flight to Berlin last April. He sat upright during the whole flight, never opened the seat belt, and time and again he would grab for the armrest. Finally, the flight attendant announced "Ladies and gentlemen, we will land at Berlin-Tegel in 10 minutes." Eric's neighbor in the next seat leaned back and sighed "Finally we've arrived." Eric turned to his neighbor and quickly replied "No, we haven't landed yet!"

This is an everyday experience. Eric's neighbor heard the announcement and right away the image of home popped into his head. He saw the plane cruising on the ground toward the gate, friends and family waiting. He was relieved. Ah, what are 10 minutes and 1500 meters above the ground? Eric had a much different image: The fact is, we are still 1500 meters above the ground, we have not yet landed, and statistics say that many plane accidents happen during landing on the last 1000 meters.

The same stimulus can create very different images. Some prefer sensing perception, others prefer intuition.

Imagine: You stand there, the door opens, and your colleagues come out of the conference room. "How was the meeting?" you ask one of them. "Well," he answers, "we started promptly at 9 a.m., as you see it took 2 hours, and we talked the entire time about the new sales event which should take off next month, on the 15th." Then you ask another colleague "How was the meeting?" and he says, "Oh, I feel like a wet towel!"

You get clear data from the sensor; and an image from the intuitive.

The Leadership Team meets every Tuesday morning. Cup of coffee in his hand, Joe Brand walks up to the conference table and picks up the report. With one hand, he turns the pages. With a professional glance he takes a look at facts and figures, points his thumb, and mumbles "Oh, we are at 4.8 now..." and takes his seat. The meeting starts. His three col-

leagues discuss page after page, covering the components of each division. Joe is just interested in the general direction and the significance of the numbers. In the meantime, Joe's mind wanders. He "knows" the result already, and plans his short vacation in his mind as he looks kind of absent-minded and uninterested (unfortunately, so interpreted by his fellow leaders). And the result was not four point eight, of course, but 4.73.

The different personalities are felt – at the CEO level and in the facility management group. And such differences are not interpreted value-free (what type theory demands). Rather they are judged by personal impressions, which often lead to friction. In the case of Joe Brand, they lead to separation – with a golden parachute, of course.

Francis heard about type theory, self-assessed herself, validated the result, and found it to be helpful. Now, at age 53, she saw many differences between herself and her husband in a different light. She definitely saw her preference for intuition (her husband was an S-type par excellence). And Francis reflected why she had downgraded her natural preference for intuition. And she remembered: When she went to school, during those first weeks as a little girl in that small town, her mother asked her quite often, "Francis, how did you get home?" "Well, I don't know." She knew her mother wanted to know exactly which streets and which corners – in detail, and in honest care. So, the next few days, intuitive Francis learned the names of the streets. And because of her parent's preference, she was injected with a prejudice that "S" is better than "N."

Such happens in life. Preference judgements are personalized and impacts are huge. Later in life it is difficult to reassess and recalibrate our perceptions of self and stand up for our true self.

If we are sensitive to personal preferences, we can then adjust our communication and save time, energy, feelings, and futures. We can learn how to create synergies among the differences.

The boss tells his employee on December 16: "Go down to the hardware store and buy 8 wooden stars, well, I think they are 4 inches in diameter, and buy 4 wooden angels about the same size. We also need some string – 15 meters will be enough; and 200 red and green beads – 100 of each color." And the employee goes to the store and can't remember ("Was it 4 wooden stars?"). The employee's preference is iNtuition and at this point he is lost.

What does the employee need? First, he needs a big picture: A Christmas tree – 6 to 7 feet tall. The employee is supposed to purchase the decorations. If he knows that, he can handle the purchase of the decorations.

4 Basic Functions and Attitudes 19

S-type spelunkers, as they explore the cave with their flashlight fixed to their helmets, have their beam of light shine right in front of them – they see the little rocks. They walk carefully and find the safest place to step. What they don't see is the precipice 10 yards ahead. The N-types, holding their heads up to see the future, see the precipice and issue warnings – but then they often stumble over that small outcropping of rock right in front of them.

Are you attending to the things directly in your path? Or do you prefer to look ahead and expectedly discover new things in your future?

S-Type
Reads instructions,
notices detail

N-Type
Skips directions,
follows hunches

S-Type
Prefers handling
practical matters

N-Type
Prefers imagining
possibilities

20 Understanding the Dynamics of Typical People

S-Type
Sees specific parts
and pieces

N-Type
Sees patterns
and relationships

S-Type
Likes things that are
definite, measurable

N-Type
Likes opportunities
to be inventive

4 Basic Functions and Attitudes 21

S-Type
Starts at the beginning,
takes a step at a time

N-Type
Jumps in anywhere,
leaps over steps

S-Type
Lives in the present,
enjoys what is there

N-Type
Lives in the future,
anticipating what might be

22 Understanding the Dynamics of Typical People

S-Type	N-Type
S-Types are often	N-Types are often
seen by N-Types	seen by S-Types
as bean counters	as dreamers

Characteristics	
Sensing	**iNtuition**
Experience	Hunch
Details	Patterns
Present	Future
Practical	Imaginative
Facts	Fiction
Sequential	Incidental
Repetition	Multiplicity
Pleasure	Expectation
Realistic	Speculative
Factual	Possible
Usefulness	Fantasy
Keep your feet on the ground	Jack-of-all-trades

Here is one more story highlighting differences in perceiving: You all know Sherlock Holmes and Watson. They had just finished a difficult case. Of course they were successful, but they were tired and decided to take a quick camping trip. They packed their gear and headed for the country. They found a beautiful camp site, pitched their tent, and built a fire. They relaxed, visited, drank wine, and ate their sandwiches. They then crawled into the tent and fell asleep.

Late into the night Holmes woke Watson, whispering "Watson, Watson, what do you see?" Waking slowly, Watson replied "I see stars, millions and millions of stars." Holmes continued: "What else do you see?" Watson said "I see stars, and among the stars I can see constellations Pisces, Aries, Taurus… and I see galaxies…" "What else do you see?" questioned Holmes. "I see the beauty and wonder of the glorious universe in which we live" responded Watson. Then Watson turned to Homes and asked; "Holmes, what do you see?" Holmes replied; "I see that someone has stolen our tent."

You see, just perception here – no judgements. When Holmes questioned Watson he was looking only for perceptions. And that is what he got, although Watson's perceptions were quite different from his own. Now we turn our attention to judging.

4.2 Judging Functions: Thinking and Feeling

How do you make decisions? How do you come to conclusions after taking in all that information and all those impressions? How do you structure all of that information that you have collected with your preferred perceiving function?

There are two processes for decision making: Objective thinking (T) that employs an impersonal, logical style based on analysis and principles, and subjective value-based feeling (F) that refers to personal values and social morés. Both thinking and feeling are logical approaches – but based on different logics. The Thinking process is an objective, linear logic; feeling is a subjective, non-linear logic.

Thinkers prefer objective, impersonal considerations, seek for truth, and are good at analysis. Feelers prefer personal considerations, seek relationship and harmony, and are good at understanding people.

The thinker needs to keep distance to be "objective." The feeler empathizes to understand the "subjective." The thinking type prefers strategies – people

T-Type
Decides with head

F-Type
Decides with heart

should be reasonable and understand it so they can follow. The feeling type would like first to include people – and will change strategies if they are not heart-felt.

Mark and his brother were contemplating the purchase of a meat market. They had done all of the cost analysis, market studies, and financial planning. Everything looked very promising. They were excited by the potential and were going to finalize the purchase on Tuesday at noon. On Tuesday morning, Mark called his brother, and said "It does not feel right to make this purchase." That ended all discussion.

In some instances, all the data in the world does not add up to a positive feeling.

T-Type
Likes logic

F-Type
Prefers personal convictions

T-Type
Concerned for truth and justice

F-Type
Concern for relationships harmony

4 Basic Functions and Attitudes

T-Type
Spontaneously criticizes
finds flaws

F-Type
Spontaneously
appreciates

Using your understanding of type preferences, what preference would appear in most software engineers given the logical technical demand of their chosen profession? Yes, engineers prefer thinking (confirmed by numerous frequency distributions).

> *We were quite surprised to find a software engineering firm crowded with Feeling types. Our assumption was that the boss who had a Feeling preference had cloned himself. When asked how they arrive at final decisions, everything was explained. Most decisions and certainly the important ones are made by consensus. They are passionate about their cause, they love it when others appreciate their work, and they make most decisions based on what they like and how it impacts others. This was clear. It was also interesting to see how a minority Thinking colleague was unable to get a foot in the door when he presented a matrix organization in his logical principled-driven way.*

More drama: This feeling-oriented organization just bought another software firm in a nearby town. The software engineers in the new organization were as expected: A much more traditional thinking culture. It was obvious to a "type watcher" that miscommunications and misunderstandings between the two organizations were on the horizon. Unfortunately, there was no opportunity for us to discuss these potential difficulties with the new owners. We later learned that within less than a year after the initial purchase, they had in turn resold the other organization. We were not surprised, knowing the statistics and reasons for merger and acquisition failures.

Again, what is the typical engineer according to frequency distribution? Thinking, of course.

> *In 1958, Ford motor company introduced the Edsel. The Edsel boasted the most modern technology designed by the best engineers in the world.*

While being well-engineered and reliable, the Edsel became perhaps the most spectacular failure in car history. Why? Because the Feeling perspective was not strategically applied in the design. Most salespeople have a Feeling preference and they know that more issues play roles in successful selling than just perfect technology. The Edsel, with its trademark "horsecollar" grille, made it distinct from other cars of the period, but also produced a widely circulated wisecrack at that "the Edsel looked like an Oldsmobile sucking on a lemon." In addition, cultural critics have speculated that the car was a flop because the vertical grill looked like a vagina. Maybe. America in the 1950s was certainly phobic about the female business.

These are clearly subjective, feeling perspectives that sank the Edsel. The thinking engineering was sound.

Perhaps Volkswagen learned from Edsel:

A few years ago, Volkswagen had Americans singing (yes, singing) Fahrvergnügen (driving pleasure or delight) with a very successful ad campaign where men and women in the commercials were singing Fahrvergnügen. Americans sang along, not even knowing the meaning of the word. That did not matter. The advertisement was created to capture the "hearts" of the buyer and did not even mention solid "German engineering." It was a very successful approach.

We all have the capacity to make decisions based on objective thinking, as well as on subjective feeling. But can we do both when necessary? There are many times that decisions impact a wide audience and it is wise to have both the clear logic of the thinking type as well as the value position of the feeling type.

A manager invited his employees for company dinner – excellent hotel, first-class cooking, everything properly styled. Afterwards, the manager reflected on the stiff, rather formal atmosphere that seemed present at the tables that evening. When asked "What would the people have said, if you had asked them personally what they would prefer for a benefit-dinner gala?" his immediate answer was "Put up a tent, get a band, and have a grill." "Why didn't you do that?" he was asked. He stammered: "Well,... I thought..."

Yes, he thought. He should also have felt a bit more.

4 Basic Functions and Attitudes

T-Type
Likes logic

F-Type
Prefers personal
convictions

T-Type
Takes a long-range
perspective

F-Type
Takes an immediate
personal view

T-Type
T-Types are often seen
by F-Types as cold and aloof

F-Type
F-Types are often seen
by T-Types as fickle and too emotional

Characteristics	
Thinking	**Feeling**
Head	Heart
Objective	Subjective
Evaluate critically	Devote oneself
Laws	Circumstances
Impersonal	Personal
Criteria	Intimacy
Critique	Positive evaluation
Stay firm	To allow to be convinced
Analyze	Empathize
Precise	Convincing
Principles	Personal values
Axiom	Social values

When making decisions, it is wise to start with your preferred function. Then quickly ask someone with your nonpreferred function to review your decision. Each decision should stand up to the objective analysis of the thinking type as well as be embraced by the values of the feeling type.

4.3 Attitude Toward Outer or Inner World: Extraversion (E) and Introversion (I)

Where do you receive your energy?

> *Bert was the director of a nonprofit organization. Maybe he had read a book about managers or had visited a seminar on leadership at some point. Anyway, he started to leave his office door open. When asked about it, he said "I want my employees to know that they can come in anytime and talk to me. But no one has stepped in to talk." Bert was a good boss, but by the way he worked everyone knew he was reserved – introverted. Anyone that merely passed by his office detected that he was concentrating and focusing on his work. People can sense that. We recommended: "Why don't you keep your door shut, then you will not get distracted and you can get your work done more quickly and then make specific appointments with your people." He tried it, and he felt much better.*

The mandate to keep your doors open is a natural request from extraverts. It works well for them, but not necessarily so for introverts.

Of course, everybody needs to withdraw from time to time – to close the doors and get things done. Introverts receive their energy while they reflect and think through issues on their own, in solitary union with themselves. They signal not to talk all the time; they need some time to reflect. Extraverts, on the other hand, get their energy as they connect with their environment. The extraverted motto is: How can I know what I think, if I don't hear what I say?

An extraverted CEO once noted: "You know, I need that walk through the woods just on my own!"

Sure, as she walks down the path by herself she looks around, enjoys nature, hears the birds singing, and takes in the smells of the forest and fauna. She is connected with the outer world and recharges her batteries. The introvert, on the other hand, might walk through the same woods, thinking, reflecting, and suddenly look up to realize that they have missed an important turn in the path.

When the extravert walks through the woods, they enjoy the trees and the landscape. The introvert loves to dive into his inner world when taking the same walk.

Introverts get their energy from their rich resources of ideas and thoughts and inner images. Extraverts act when they are confronted with a new challenge. Introverts, on the other side, seem to shy away and withdraw.

Obviously, many assessment centers exhibit a bias. More than once we have seen potential leaders after they had gone through a standard assessment center where they had been challenged on the spot to react or present an idea. Who is at a disadvantage from the very beginning? Yes, the introvert.

Joanne is an IT expert. She worked diligently on a programming project. On Thursday afternoon she finally found the solution she had been looking for over the past week. And she expressed her relief. Her colleague looked up and said "Oh, I am working on a similar problem with the same kind of solution – and got it solved yesterday afternoon." When asked why she (Joanne) didn't share the solution with her colleague because then time would have been spent much more efficiently, she responded by suggesting the development of a matrix where colleagues could see who is working on which problem and share insights as they progressed. None of her colleagues were interested in the face-to-face communication process. As a matter of fact, they were all introverts in Joanne's department. They preferred communication on their own terms – preferring closed doors so they can concentrate and, of course, enjoying a coffee break together (in a small group).

And the extraverts? Just talkers? Not necessarily. Consider the lady at the bank. She prefers extraversion. Naturally, she has to concentrate on her work. Her desk is right at the window. "I have a great job – three days in the office, and two days on the road with the sales team. And when I lose psychic energy sitting at my desk, I just look out the window and enjoy the traffic and the people out there – just for a few minutes – and I get my energy back."

Andrew prefers extraversion. He had written a book and needed to be on the road to do the promotion thing. The day he came back to the office after a 3-week tour, the staff greeted him in mass – he just asked for his mail, said he was tired and wanted to go back to his apartment. After 15 minutes relaxing at home, he realized he had forgotten some things at the office. So he walked back again, opened the door, smelled the coffee, saw all of his colleagues – and for the next 2 hours they talked.

The difference between extraverts and introverts: For the extravert, the ceiling comes down quicker when they are alone. They get their energy when they talk to others.

What preferences do actors have? Extravert? Of course, there are many actors who prefer extraversion. But there is the anecdote about the introverted Austrian actor Peter Weck:

On stage he got stuck – forgot his lines. The prompter gave the next line. Peter Weck had no reaction. The prompter repeated the line (the first few rows could hear). His colleagues behind stage stopped and looked at him. Peter Weck still had no reaction. Then he said: "No details, please. What is the name of the play?"

He is an introvert. If an introvert loses the connection to the role stored inside of him, he loses the train of thought. An extravert could have talked on until he was back on track, but not so for the introvert. There are different strategies for extraverts and introverts to load up their batteries for psychic energy.

E-Type
Is energized
by others

I-Type
Is energized
by inner resources

4 Basic Functions and Attitudes   **31**

E-Type
Feels pulled outward
by external claims and conditions

I-Type
Feels pushed inward
by external claims and conditions

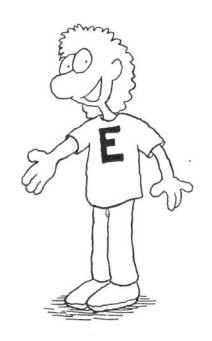

E-Type
Is often friendly,
talkative, easy to know

I-Type
Is reserved,
quiet, hard to know

E-Type
Needs relationships

I-Type
Needs privacy

E-Type
Expresses emotions

I-Type
Withholds emotions

E-Type
Gives breadth to life

I-Type
Gives depth to life

E-Type
E-Types are often seen by I-Types as "superficial" and not well grounded

I-Type
I-Types are often seen by E-Types as isolated and difficult to get to know

4 Basic Functions and Attitudes

Characteristics	
Extraversion	**Introversion**
Acting	Reflecting
Focused external	Focused internal
Contacting	Concentrating
Accessible	Reserved
Outward	Inward
Speaker	Listener
Much	Little
Expressive	Quiet
Breadth	Depth
Excessive	Intensive
Outer world	Inner world

Source of energy: Extraversion or introversion. Where do you get your energy?

4.4 Lifestyle (Attitude Toward Outside World): Judging and Perceiving

Each person takes a different attitude or posture when dealing with the outside world. According to type theory, there is a preference for either judging, structuring, and looking for clear patterns (J), or for perceiving and adapting to the situation (P). The judging type is more result oriented; the perceiving type is more process oriented. The judging type needs a plan, wants to organize or have instructions what to do when and where. The perceiving type is open for new insights or aspects, wants to stay open-minded, and prefers options. In a team environment, different people with preferences for judging or perceiving might get on each others' nerves. People who live and work together with the different attitudes can learn to accept and appreciate each other – actually the key learning with typology.

> The first step in a traditional workshop is the agenda, which is quite a challenge for those with a judging preference when the leader opens the workshop without structure and invites participants to "just start and see where we go…"

> *On the other hand, in a meeting with more than 50 people at 9:15 a.m., the moderator started out with a clear-cut schedule. Two hours later one of the participants commented "When you started out this morning, I thought I was in the wrong meeting – we were supposed to meet each*

other and share, the schedule felt like a noose around my neck. But now, I must say, things are going quite well."

Try not to quickly type people on first sight. Sometimes we have to look beyond the surface. Consider the caricature below:

Upon entering that cleaned-up office, if you ask the person on the left for the keys to the company car and he starts looking, searching all over, moving papers, going through desk drawers, and finally calls his wife to check his trousers back home lying under the bed, then you know you are dealing with a P. And when you enter the office of the person on the right and ask for the minutes of the meeting 5 weeks ago, and he pulls out the right document from the left pile, you could type him as a J.

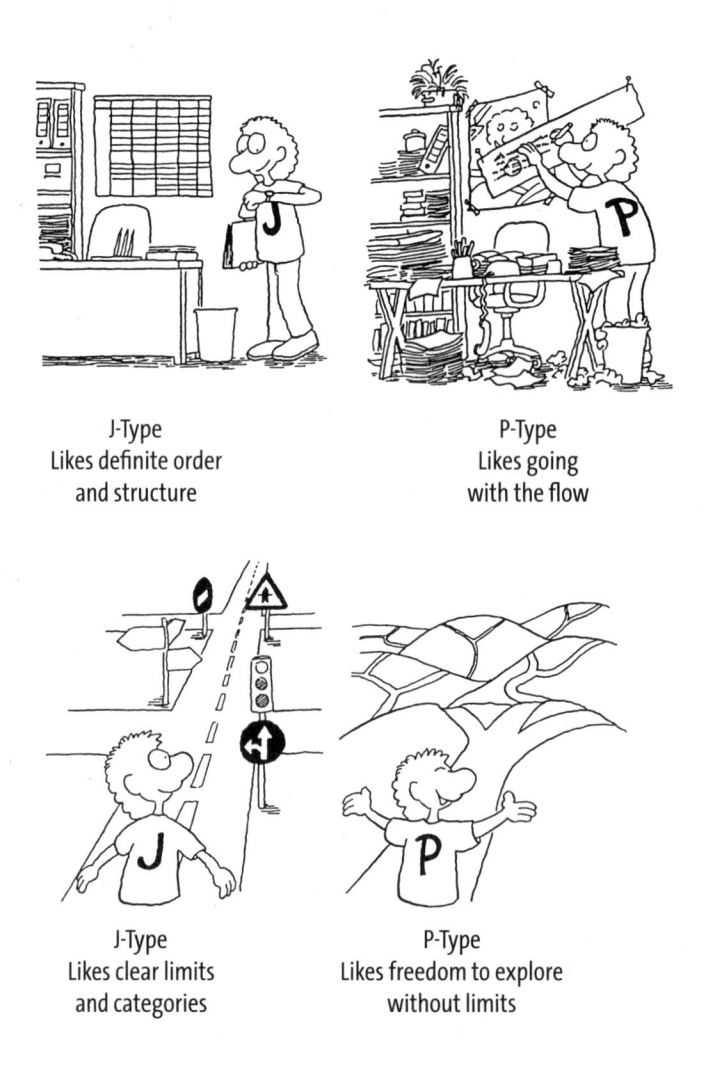

J-Type
Likes definite order
and structure

P-Type
Likes going
with the flow

J-Type
Likes clear limits
and categories

P-Type
Likes freedom to explore
without limits

4 Basic Functions and Attitudes 35

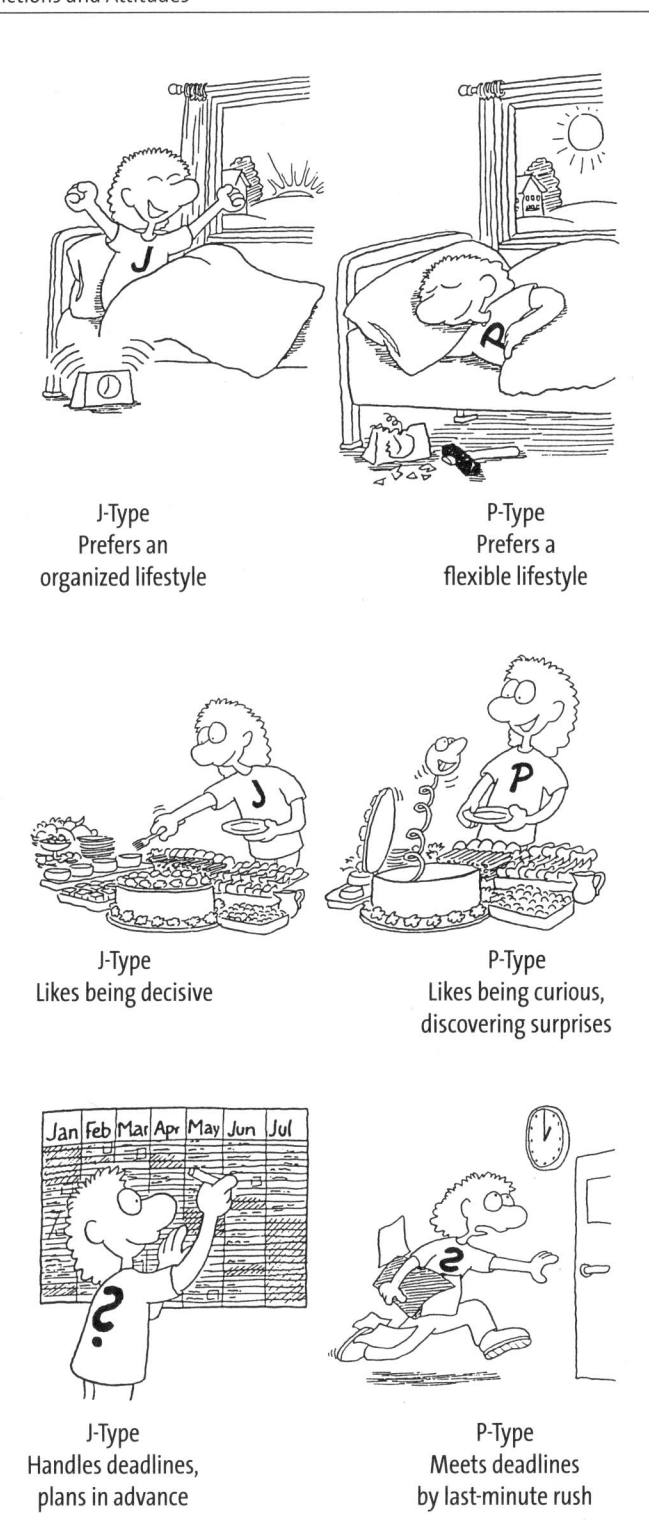

J-Type
Prefers an
organized lifestyle

P-Type
Prefers a
flexible lifestyle

J-Type
Likes being decisive

P-Type
Likes being curious,
discovering surprises

J-Type
Handles deadlines,
plans in advance

P-Type
Meets deadlines
by last-minute rush

36 Understanding the Dynamics of Typical People

J-Type
Likes closure,
completed tasks

P-Type
Prefers openness
and enjoys the process

J-Type
Looking at the J-Type
the P-Types often find them
over-organized and structured

P-Type
Looking at the P-Type
the J-Types often find them
unorganized and being in a muddle

Characteristics	
Judging	**Perceiving**
Established	Floating
Organized	Flexible
Decision	More information
Structure	Flowing
Control	Experience
Decisive	Expectant
Systematic	Spontaneous
Closure	Openness
Plan	Adjustment
Appointments	Discoveries
Concluded	Emerging
Productive	Receptive
Product	Process

Some people prefer an organized result. Others prefer an open, flexible process. And where do you stand?

4.5 Validation

You now know a bit about type. As you read the last pages you probably tried to see where you fit best. It is always important to validate your type. Even if you have taken a survey or inventory, double checking and verifying the results can sharpen your self image. Please complete the following:
1. First, what is your preferred attitude – extravert (E) or introvert (I)? Choose one of those two letters and write it in the first place below.
2. What is your preference for perceiving the world – via senses (S) or intuition (N)? Choose one of these letters and write it in the second place below.
3. What is your preferred way of decision making – analytical (T) or value-driven (F)? Choose one of these letters and write it in the third place below.
4. Finally, what is your attitude toward the outer world – do you prefer clear structures (J) or do you prefer looking at things as they come, perceiving (P)? Choose one these letters and write it in the last place.

____(1)____ ____(2)____ ____(3)____ ____(4)____

This is your preferred type as you see it at this point. The validation ought to continue. We will offer a bit more in that context.

5 Type Dynamics

Type dynamics is the interaction of our functions and attitudes. Type dynamics gives further differentiation to our personality. It explains us at a deeper level. It also underscores our development path. There are "typical" or normal patterns to personality development and Jung's type theory exposes these patterns. We all grow and change in some typical ways.

Each person prefers one of the two perceiving functions (either sensing or intuition) and one of the judging functions (thinking or feeling). These two dimensions – perceiving and judging – are the core of personality. You will find them in the middle two letters of your four-letter type code.

Using the four function letters (S, N, T, F), four possible combinations are possible: ST, SF, NF, NT. One of the letters in these two-letter combinations is dominant and the other is secondary (auxiliary). The dominant is most preferred, most trusted, and imparts high self-confidence (because one has practiced how to use it). The dominant function is likely to be evident earliest in life because it is differentiated first during childhood. The secondary or auxiliary function typically becomes more evident (*differentiated*) during teenage years and provides balance to the dominant function. The secondary function supports the dominant function. They work together in harmony (with the secondary always in a subordinate position) to give you perception and decision-making preferences. In your four-letter preference type, one of the middle two letters will be your dominant function and the other will be your auxiliary function.

Obviously, we are more than just our preferences. Less-preferred functions are part of our personality as well. They are not ignored. It is just that as we observe personality, it is the preferences that are most identifiable. It is important to know that for each of our preferences, there is a bipolar opposite that plays a role in our personality as well. When a person has a clear personality profile, we point out again that there is nothing like a pure ST, SF, NF, or NT type. Everyone finds a contingent of each function within themselves. Type indicators serve to assist in the identification of the dominant function within that complex interaction of psychic processes. All four dimensions are present in our personality, and they are influenced dramatically by the identifiable preferences.

In normal development, individuals tend to become more fluent with nonpreferred functions – a third, tertiary function during midlife, and a fourth, inferior function that remains least consciously developed and will probably never be fully differentiated. This fourth, inferior function is often considered to be more

5 Type Dynamics

associated with the subconscious. It is most evident in situations such as high stress (sometimes referred to as being *in the grip* of the inferior function).

The sequence of differentiation of dominant, secondary, and tertiary functions through life is commonly called type development. Note that this is a "normal" sequence of development that may be disrupted by major life events.

Graphically, type development according to Jung looks like this:

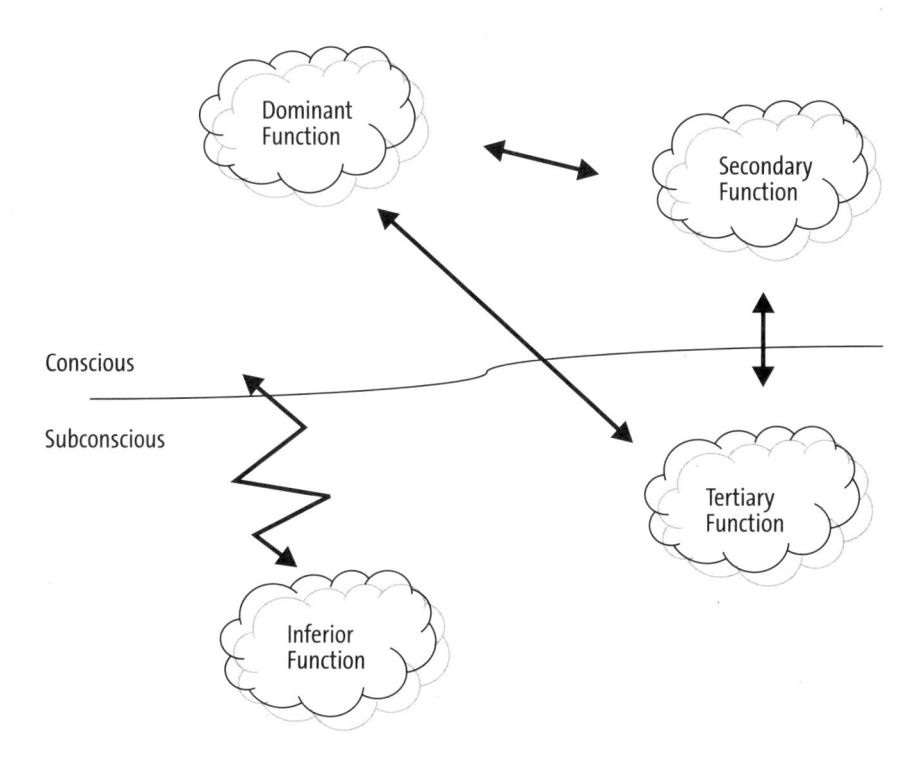

```
                    Dominant                    Secondary
                    Function  ←——→              Function

                                                    ↕
Conscious  ─────────────────────────────────
Subconscious                                    Tertiary
                                                Function

                    Inferior
                    Function
```

There is clear and conscious interaction between the dominant and secondary function. This is clear early in life. The interaction among the dominant, secondary, and tertiary function becomes conscious later – sometime during midlife. And the inferior function becomes conscious only on occasion and then retreats back to the subconscious.

As you read the next sections, continue to look for patterns, bipolarity, and harmony. These are part of the strength of Jungian typology. The following process does not simplify Jung's complex processes, but rather it points to development and sources that a person can exercise in concrete situations. All psychological functions and attitudes interact dynamically among and within each other. They allow delight and determine frustration in everyday life. If you are conscious of your own dynamics, you have a much better chance to focus and support your personal development.

5.1 Dominant Function for Extraverted Types (E)

To determine the dominate function, we turn to our attitudes: The first letter (E/I) and last letter (J/P) of our four-letter-code. As stated earlier, the first letter (E or I) points to the preference of psychic energy – the outer world or the inner world. The last letter (J or P) identifies preference for structure or perception. The attitudes normally are easy to identify. They serve to identify that what we call the "core of personality": Our dominant, auxiliary, tertiary, and inferior functions.

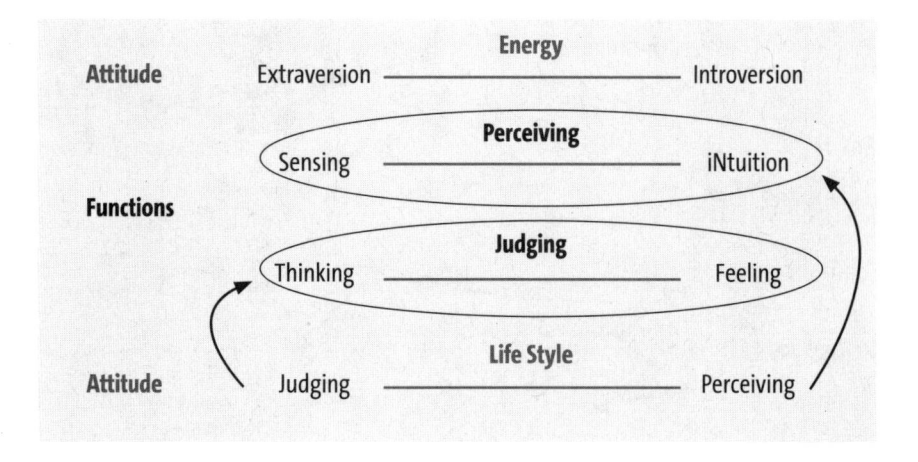

		Energy	
Attitude	Extraversion	———————————	Introversion
		Perceiving	
	Sensing	———————————	iNtuition
Functions			
		Judging	
	Thinking	———————————	Feeling
		Life Style	
Attitude	Judging	———————————	Perceiving

First, the extraverts (they like to be first, putting themselves out into the world and finding their energy out there). According to definition, extraverts are easy to identify. And to find their dominant function we merely look at the last letter (J or P). The last letter of an extraverted type will point directly to the dominant function. That is: *If an extravert reports "P," then the perceiving function (sensing or intuition) is the dominant characteristic.* For example, the dominant function of an ESTP is sensing (S), and the dominant function of an ENFP is intuition (N).

If perceiving (S or N) is the dominant for an extraverted type, then judging (T or F) will be the secondary, auxiliary, or supporting function. Take the ESTP: Dominant function is sensing (S) and secondary is thinking (T). For the ENFP-type intuition, (N) is dominant and feeling (F) is secondary.

On the other hand, if the last letter of an extravert is "J," then judging is dominant. For example, the dominant function of ESFJ is feeling (F). The rule for extraverts is: The last letter points to the dominant function.

Put another way, the overall *lifestyle preference* (J–P) identifies whether the judging (T–F) or perceiving (S–N) preference is most evident in the outside world, i.e., which function has an extraverted attitude. A common rule here is that "we use our favorite function in our favorite world." The extravert claims the outer world as favorite, therefore they display their dominant function in that world.

5 Type Dynamics   **41**

For those with an overall preference for extraversion, the function with the *extraverted attitude* will be the dominant function. The secondary or auxiliary function for extraverts is the secondary preference of the judging or perceiving functions, and it is experienced with an introverted attitude. For example, the auxiliary function for ESTJ is introverted sensing and the auxiliary for ESTP is introverted thinking.

Again, for extravert: The last letter points to the dominant function.

5.2 Dominant Function for Introverted Types (I)

Now we turn our attention to the introvert. Introverts are not as easy to get to know. They have a tendency to be reserved and keep their thoughts, ideas and feelings more private. Only when they are in a familiar environment do they show their dominant function. To the outside world, they show their second function – they save the best for themselves or for only a few close intimate friends. That means when we look at the last letter of the type indicator of an introvert we have to remember that it points to the function which is not dominant. If the last letter of an introvert is "P," then it points to the perceiving function, which is secondary, and the judging function is dominant.

For example, the dominant function of an ISFP is value-based decision making (F), and sensing (S) is secondary. If the last letter of an introvert type is "J," then the perceiving function is dominant, and judging is secondary. For the ISTJ, sensing (S) is dominant and thinking (T) is secondary. Again, the rule: "You use your favorite function in your favorite world."

For the introvert: The last letter of the type code points to the secondary function.

In summary, for those with an overall preference for introversion, the function with the extraverted attitude is the *auxiliary*; the dominant is the other function in the main four-letter preference. So the dominant function for ISTJ is introverted sensing with the auxiliary (supporting) function being extraverted thinking.

And there is more. We are more than just our preferred functions.

5.3 Tertiary and Inferior Function

We just discussed the two preferred functions of personality: The dominant and the secondary. There are two more functions that guide and influence your personality: The tertiary and the inferior function. The inclusion of the tertiary and inferior functions provides a holistic view of personality – the preferred and the nonpreferred.

The identification of these functions is not so complex, especially if we remember that the entire theory is based on bipolarity and harmony. For example,

ISTJ: The dominant is sensing (S) according to the logic of the theory, and thinking (T) is secondary. The third function is always opposite the second function. Therefore, for ISTJ, intuition (N) is tertiary. And, of course, the fourth or inferior function is always opposite the dominant function – for the ISTJ the inferior function would be intuition (N).

The reasoning for this pattern is clear: If a person spends more time differentiating one function that becomes favored, preferred, dominant, and provides self-confidence for the person, then the opposite of that dimension remains undifferentiated. As discussed in the following chapter on stress, the inferior function serves as a channel for chaotic reactions of the brain (or the "subconscious" as Jung framed that vast shadowy part of personality). It triggers that sense of "feeling beside myself" or reactions of "blowing up."

Again, remember, the tertiary function is the opposite from the auxiliary and the inferior is always opposite the dominant.

5.4 Summary – Dynamics of Type

The first letter is your preferred source of energy:
   Extraversion or **I**ntroversion.

The second letter is your preference for perceiving:
   Sensing or i**N**tuition.

The third letter is your preferred way of making judgments:
   Thinking or **F**eeling.

The fourth letter is your preferred way of functioning in the outer world:
   Judging or **P**erceiving.

The dynamics of type focused on the functions (the middle two letters) in the four-letter type. We use the attitudes (the first and last letters) to assist in determining the dominant, secondary, tertiary, and inferior functions. How do you determine the function order?

Dominant
Secondary
Tertiary
Inferior

For extraverts: The first step is to look at the last letter in your type code; it points directly to your dominant function. For introverts: The first step is to look at the last letter in your type code; it tells you your secondary function. Or, you can just look at the chart below:

The Order of Preferences

ISTJ	ISFJ	INFJ	INTJ
Introverted Sensing (S) Extraverted Thinking (T) Extraverted Feeling (F) Extraverted Intuition (N)	Introverted Sensing (S) Extraverted Feeling (F) Extraverted Thinking (T) Extraverted Intuition (N)	Introverted Intuition (N) Extraverted Feeling (F) Extraverted Thinking (T) Extraverted Sensing (S)	Introverted Intuition (N) Extraverted Thinking (T) Extraverted Feeling (F) Extraverted Sensing (S)
ISTP	**ISFP**	**INFP**	**INTP**
Introverted Thinking (T) Extraverted Sensing (S) Extraverted Intuition (N) Extraverted Feeling (F)	Introverted Feeling (F) Extraverted Sensing (S) Extraverted Intuition (N) Extraverted Thinking (T)	Introverted Feeling (F) Extraverted Intuition (N) Extraverted Sensing (S) Extraverted Thinking (T)	Introverted Thinking (T) Extraverted Intuition (N) Extraverted Sensing (S) Extraverted Feeling (F)
ESTP	**ESFP**	**ENFP**	**ENTP**
Extraverted Sensing (S) Introverted Thinking (T) Introverted Feeling (F) Introverted Intuition (N)	Extraverted Sensing (S) Introverted Feeling (F) Introverted Thinking (T) Introverted Intuition (N)	Extraverted Intuition (N) Introverted Feeling (F) Introverted Thinking (T) Introverted Sensing (S)	Extraverted Intuition (N) Introverted Thinking (T) Introverted Feeling (F) Introverted Sensing (S)
ESTJ	**ESFJ**	**ENFJ**	**ENTJ**
Extraverted Thinking (T) Introverted Sensing (S) Introverted Intuition (N) Introverted Feeling (F)	Extraverted Feeling (F) Introverted Sensing (S) Introverted Intuition (N) Introverted Thinking (T)	Extraverted Feeling (F) Introverted Intuition (N) Introverted Sensing (S) Introverted Thinking (T)	Extraverted Thinking (T) Introverted Intuition (N) Introverted Sensing (S) Introverted Feeling (F)

The dynamics of type may be illustrated by just a few more examples. The dynamics of the ESTJ are found in the combination of extraverted thinking as the dominant function and introverted sensing as the auxiliary function. The dominant tendency of ESTJ is look to clear decisions, order their environment, set clear boundaries, clarify roles and timetables, and to direct the activities around them. This is supported by the secondary function (sensing) and the collecting of facts, attending to detail, and using past experience in an ordered and systematic way.

The ESTJ enjoys setting plans for groups of people to achieve some particular goal or to perform some focused function. "Git 'er done" is their motto. And because of their ease in directing others and their attention to managing their own time, they engage all the resources at their disposal to achieve their goals.

Although the ESTJ can seem insensitive to the feelings of others in their normal activities, when under tremendous stress they can suddenly express feelings of being unappreciated or wounded by insensitivity. At this point they are in the grip of their inferior function: Introverted feeling (more on stress and personality in the next chapters).

Another example: The dynamics of the INFP rest on the fundamental interaction of introverted feeling and extraverted intuition. The dominant tendency of the INFP is toward building a rich internal framework of values and silently working to champion human rights. They often devote themselves behind the scenes to causes in which they deeply believe. Because they prefer their inner world and tend to avoid too much outward attention while postponing decisions, and because they maintain a reserved posture, they are rarely found in executive or director positions. Normally, the INFP dislikes being "in charge" of things; they are collaborators and team players – they work toward harmony. When not under stress, the INFP radiates a pleasant and sympathetic demeanor; but under extreme stress, they can suddenly become rigid and directive, exerting their extraverted thinking erratically. More will be shared on the stress issue and the inferior function in the following chapters.

Type dynamics and the expression of these dynamics give each personality type its unique, recognizable signature. Essential to Jungian typology is that:

- Each human being is unique and distinctive. The life challenge is for every human being to explore and discover that given individuality and interact with others and the environment in an ever purposeful way.
- At the same time we discover "typical" patterns with every human being we also recognize the uniqueness of each.
- The "typical" is guided by the strength of profiled preferences, by the interaction of the two central functions, and the preferred attitudes.
- The nonpreferred functions serve a critical role as potentials for personal development and explain stress reactions in difficult circumstances.
- The key issue is holistic health of the person working toward what Jung called "completion," even using stressful experiences for promoting growth and health of the person.

Reviewing all of the type descriptions may be useful in your continued validation of your type. We suggest that, as you read these descriptions, you note the aspects that clearly resonate with how you perceive yourself. Also identify where you have questions. Validation continues.

6 Description of the Individual Types

Descriptions of each of the 16 types puts the four scales together in dynamic fashion. The descriptions are an articulation of how the bipolar scales work together in harmony. The descriptions ought to assist with your validation of type. Remember, these are generic descriptions and none of them will fit exactly. One of them will come quite close to describing your personality, however.

6.1 Short Descriptions

The following section provides an overview of the 16 types. Read the short description of what you believe to be your type and see how well it fits. Take your time and carefully read the type description; validate your self-assessment. If the description does not quite describe your preference, exchange the letter that you were unsure of and then read that type description. You are looking for the best fit – the one that fits you better than any of the other 15 types. The validation continues, as does your learning about yourself and others.

ISTJ	ISFJ
You are a no-nonsense individual who is exceedingly dependable. Logic and handwork are valued. You are serious, quiet, practical, orderly, matter-of-fact, and realistic. You earn your success by concentration and thoroughness, and see to it that everything is well organized. Taking responsibility is natural for you.	Conscientious, friendly, quiet, and responsible, you work devotedly to meet obligations. You provide stability; others know they can trust you to be thorough and painstakingly accurate. You are patient with detail and routine. You are loyal, considerate, concerned with how other people feel. You tend to remember facts about people and relationships.
ISTP	**ISFP**
A cool onlooker, quiet, reserved, you observe and analyze life with detached curiosity. You are usually interested in impersonal principles, cause and effect, how and why things work. You often become wholly absorbed, even single-minded, when trying to solve a problem. You are able objectively to avoid distractions that might get in your way	Cheerful, lighthearted, warm, and sensitive, you are quietly kind and modest. You tend to shun disagreements and do not force your opinions or values on others. Loyal and often relaxed about getting things done while savoring the present moment, you do not want to spoil it by undue haste or exertion. You often accurately praise others for their unique talents.
ESTP	**ESFP**
You see the world as it is, approach it with curiosity, observe it well, and embrace it openly. Matter-of-fact, you enjoy whatever comes along. Adaptable, tolerant, generally conservative in values. Work frequently becomes play, you thrive on action and are good in a crisis. You like clear short explanations, and are best with real tactile things.	Cheerful, outgoing, living happily with and meeting others, the here and now are important to you and you like actual experience and real people. You join in the fun eagerly. Remembering facts is easier for you than mastering theories. You are best in situations that demand common sense and practical ability with people as well as with things.
ESTJ	**ESFJ**
Objective, practical, realistic, matter-of-fact, you are a natural organizer of your entire environment. You like to plan and organize things with clear goals and timelines. Routine and repetition create mastery – you are a good administrator, straightforward in your views and expect others to be the same. Past experience is helpful in solving problems.	Warm-hearted, talkative, popular, collaborative - your values and need to promote harmony are at the forefront of everything you do. Harmony is necessary and you are good at creating it while always doing something nice for someone. You work best with praise and specific encouragement. Your main interests are in things that visibly affect people's lives.

INFJ	**INTJ**
You live in a world of ideas, succeed by perseverance, originality. You desire to do whatever is needed or wanted. You are an imaginative, inspired, tenacious, creative, and inward-looking individual. Quietly forceful, conscientious, and concerned for others, you are respected for your firm principles. You are likely to be honored for your clear convictions.	Pure ideas, vast and complex give you identity. Your original mind drives you toward your own original goals and purposes. You tend to be skeptical, critical, independent, determined, and hold to your ideals. You approach any and every situation as an inventor, innovator, organizer, and reviser.
INFP	**INTP**
You are capable of immense sensitivity and have enormous emotional capacity, which you closely guard. You tend to be enthusiastic and loyal. Learning, ideas, language, and independent projects appeal to you. You demonstrate little concern with possessions or physical surroundings. Harmony is essential in your personal life and you seek to promote peace.	Quiet, reserved, impersonal, you value rational thought over all things. No problem is so complex that it cannot be thought through. You enjoy the theoretical and are logical to the point of hairsplitting. Ideas are supreme and you tend to have sharply defined interests. Your objective thought combines with your continuous flow of imaginative ideas.
ENFP	**ENTP**
Warm, enthusiastic, high-spirited, ingenious, imaginative, you possess an almost magnetic quality that allows you to have fun in almost any setting and an ability to do most anything that interests you. You are quick with a solution for any difficulty and ready to help anyone with a problem. Improvisation prepares you in advance with compelling reasons for whatever you want.	Highly vibrant with a finger on the pulse of the future you are quick, ingenious, and good at many things. Logically you may argue on either side of the question. Visionary and explorative, you see the big picture and do not get caught up in messy details. You revel in solving challenging problems, and are apt to turn to one new interest after another.
ENFJ	**ENTJ**
Responsive and responsible, you seek to ensure harmony and bliss between yourself and others. You generally feel real concern for what others think or want, and try to handle things with due regard for others' feelings. You lead with ease and tact. Relationships are important; you are sociable, popular, and sympathetic. You appreciate praise and constructive criticism.	Your ultimate desire is to lead, to be frank, decisive, strategic. You are usually good at anything that requires reasoning and intelligent approaches. You enjoy long-range planning and your vision allows you to spot potential pitfalls far ahead. Making tough-minded decisions does not scare you. You are rarely content to sit back quietly and watch.

6.2 Description of the 16 Types

There are 16 distinct personality types according to Jung. Each type has its own characteristics that can be identified in individual personalities. We have created a profile of each personality type, which provides a guideline for understanding the similarities and differences among the types.

Starting with a description of each type, we then provide a list of ways that each particular type contributes to an organization, their preferred leadership style, and the way each type is likely to communicate. We also identify motivators and demotivators for each type, how the type functions in a group, their preferred learning style, and suggested opportunities for growth.

This is yet another opportunity for validation of your type. How closely do you align with the type description and the designated characteristics?

ENFP – Extraverted/iNtuitive/Feeling/Perceiving

ENFPs are individuals who live continually in the realm of the possible. When absorbed in your latest project, you think of little else. Your energy level is sometimes exhausting to behold. You are virtually tireless in the pursuit of your latest goal as long as your interest in the project holds. Your infectious commitment and self-confidence allows you to have many devoted followers.

Of all the personality types, an ENFP possesses an almost magnetic quality that allows you to have fun in almost any setting. Your combination of Extraversion, Intuition, and Perceiving equips you well to be a leader. You have a natural ability to understand others, to figure out what motivates them, and to appreciate their unique qualities without judging or criticizing. ENFPs approach an amazing variety of problems with ease, and the diversity of your interests is mirrored by the diversity of your friends. In fact, diversity is the universal key to happiness in your life. You focus much of your energy on developing and understanding who you are, identifying your goals, and building meaningful relationships with others. It is important for you to be an authentic person, to be in touch with yourself and, therefore, to be capable of really touching others.

Frequently, ENFPs have the feeling of being on the brink of a great discovery about people or life. Your intuition gathers information from the real world and then mixes it with imagination to synthesize a unique view of reality. You are your own person in every sense. It is difficult to awe you with sterile rank and titles. As an ENFP you are an optimistic, independent soul, who believes in yourself when no one else does. In the long run, you will be wise to opt for a career and relationships that allow flexibility and include the companionship of other creative, like-minded souls who also reject structure for its own sake and admire ideas for their intrinsic worth.

ENFP
Contributions to an organization – you:
- Are spontaneous and provide imaginative answers;
- Easily see and grasp all future possibilities;
- Welcome change and often are a catalyst for it;
- Have the versatility to excel in many different types of tasks;
- Enjoy troubleshooting people problems;
- Bring positive attitudes, passion, and ongoing inspiration;
- Easily spot interpersonal fakes, scams, or destructiveness;
- Give praise and acknowledgment to those with whom you interact.

Leadership style – you:
- Provide enthusiasm and step in when visionary leadership is required;
- Develop personal relationships with coworkers rather than using a hands-off, task-oriented management or leadership approach;
- Accept risk, particularly if people will benefit;

- Bring together the variety of people, resources, commitments, and programs;
- Focus on areas of agreement but easily negotiate differences among members so everyone can get back to a harmonious environment;
- Lead with the belief that leadership and authority is granted by integrity, not position.

Communication style preferences – you:
- Speak with energy and excitement;
- Reply quickly with impromptu responses;
- Talk in person rather than communicating in writing;
- Use lively, vivid imagery and words;
- See the big picture and typically present that first;
- Share your unique insights through unusual approaches;
- Persuade others with emotionally presented material;
- Share personal experience to make a point.

Motivators and demotivators – you:
- Seek variety, challenge, diversity, novelty, and new ideas;
- Want opportunities to express yourself and to grow and learn;
- Appreciate being affirmed, acknowledged, and recognized;
- Desire opportunities to use your insights for the good of all;
- Love to put out people-fires and create last-minute improvisations;
- Avoid situations where people are not allowed to participate.

As part of a group – you:
- Contribute creative ideas along with humanitarian values;
- Are terrific at integrating people, resources, and overall vision;
- Prefer to concentrate on the larger picture;
- Can sometimes lead the team off-track because you see so many possibilities in a project;
- Are are irritated by team members who think negatively or see through a small lens;
- Are an optimist about time schedules and workload, sometimes promising more than what is reasonable or "doable";
- Are irritated by team members who do not respect others.

Your learning style includes:
- Preference for lessons that are adventurous and creative;
- A need for time to explore possibilities, ask questions, and use imagination;
- Learning through a variety of methods;
- A dislike of narrow structure or straight lectures;
- Excelling when the teacher or facilitator takes a personal interest in you.

Suggested opportunities for growth – you should:
- Avoid getting too deeply involved in the personal needs of others;
- Practice setting goals; you should carefully choose a particular course of action that you can commit to, and then stay on course until it is completed;
- Pay more attention to details and routines;
- Not take criticism personally; you should turn it into useful feedback for personal growth;
- Pause and reflect first before bounding off in another direction – others can get easily frustrated by your ENFP tendency to switch gears in midstream.

ENFJ – Extraverted/iNtuitive/Feeling/Judging

As an ENFJ your chief concern is fostering harmony and cooperation between yourself and others. You have strong ideals and a potent sense of loyalty, whether to an employer, a mate, a school, a hometown, or a favorite cause. You tend to give generously and work tirelessly to make things perfect for your family, your home, and your place of employment. You are usually good at organizing people to get things done while keeping everyone happy at the same time.

You will find that you are well equipped to deal with both variety and action. Disorganized situations frequently strike you as chaotic. You may be uncomfortable when obliged to function without a schedule, plan, or clear idea of the objectives to be achieved. You are usually willing to take on the responsibility of planning, programming, assigning tasks, developing projects, and delegating activities. Typically patient and conscientious, ENFJs tend to make a concerted effort of sticking with a job until it is finished. When there is a discrepancy between your own performance and your ideal behavior, you may struggle with feelings of dissatisfaction or guilt. You are frequently harder on yourself than the situation warrants. The ENFJ personality type gravitates toward being an idealist and truthseeker, frequently scanning the horizon for the possibilities in a situation, always with an eye toward the application of ideas to the world of people. This ability arms you well to be a discoverer and a visionary.

Your skill as a persuasive communicator is more likely to be dedicated to speaking than to writing. Your comfort with words is illustrated by your bright language and colorful imagery. You are at your best when leading in direct, face-to-face encounters. You tend to enjoy joint ventures and excel when working with a group. Relationships are a crucial focus for you. You frequently invest your time, energy, and patience in relationships. Your personal strengths are your verbal abilities, empathy with others, and your ability to build harmony.

ENFJ

Contributions to an organization – you:
- Bring energy, warmth, enthusiasm and cooperation to tasks;
- Are a catalyst for drawing out the best in people;
- Improve technology and strive for efficiency;
- Plan carefully toward reaching goals;
- Contribute order, a positive attitude, and sociability to an organization;
- Strive to find mutually beneficial solutions and resolutions to projects;
- Easily lead others with high ethical standards;
- Bring the ideal into reality;
- Have the ability to see trends and potential pitfalls.

Leadership style – you:
- Are at your best in the role of facilitator;
- Believe work is accomplished through building relationships;

6 Description of the Individual Types

- Demand consistency between organizational goals, actions, and values;
- Enjoy hands-on participation in administering people and projects;
- Try to gauge the schedule to avoid crises, but if one occurs your focus is on the impact it will have on people;
- Inspire innovation and transformation in those you lead.

Communication style preferences – you:
Speak with energy and excitement;
Reply quickly with impromptu responses;
Talk in person, rather than communicate in writing;
Use language that is full of metaphors, analogies, and symbols;
Listen to and hear not only what is said, but also what is NOT said;
Discuss future challenges to prepare for potential problems;
Persuade by material presented with emotion or of a personal nature;
Communicate personal experiences to make points.

Motivators and demotivators – you:
- Prefer a supportive, organized, and harmonious environment;
- Require positive recognition and opportunities for self-expression;
- Prefer projects that use creativity and involve others;
- Need and want to be in the lines of communication;
- Like jobs that are not purely task-oriented;
- Are frustrated when only cold, impersonal logic is applied to a situation.

As part of a group – you:
- Are a natural leader and facilitator;
- Develop plans with the project's value or ideal in mind;
- Bring structure, organization, sensitivity, consensus, and cooperation;
- Allow team members to make mistakes and learn from their errors;
- May irritate others by focusing on personal concerns;
- Are irritated by members who disregard timelines or schedules and who are intolerant of others.

Your learning style includes:
- Performing best in a structured learning environment;
- Feeling interaction with others and discussion of the lesson to be very important;
- Learning best when you understand how the material is connected to helping people;
- Liking theories and abstractions;
- Resisting instructors/facilitators who are not warm and personable.

Suggested opportunities for growth – you should:
- Consider loyalties carefully to avoid becoming blindly loyal to a group, project, or cause;

- Realize that not everyone shares your level of devotion;
- Avoid becoming overextended and committed to other people's requests;
- Not take criticism personally – you should turn it into useful feedback for personal growth;
- Take your time when making decisions;
- Include focused details and objective information when presenting.

…

ENTP – Extraverted/iNtuitive/Thinking/Perceiving

ENTPs are highly dynamic individuals who are typically happiest living on the edge of the future. Life is one glorious game. You function continually in the realm of the possible. When absorbed in your latest project, you can think of little else. You are virtually tireless in the pursuit of your latest goal – as long as your interest holds. You approach a wide variety of problems with ease. The breadth of your interests is a strength. Diversity is the universal key to happiness in your life.

You value logic over sentiment. Sometimes it is difficult for you to appreciate how others value emotion. You do have the interpersonal skills necessary to connect with people when you want to. In tasks requiring quick decisions and fast action, you reign supreme. However, you must constantly be on guard not to act too quickly, particularly without thinking things through completely before you act. ENTPs use intuition to scan the horizon and search out the possibilities in a situation. Therefore, you are a discoverer and visionary. You are in love with learning, and are fascinated by the very concept of intelligence. You seem to have an inner drive toward performance and a highly self-critical nature that continually drives you toward self-improvement.

ENTPs are supremely self-confident. Your intellectual ability provides the substance needed to accomplish virtually anything you wish for in life. Most likely, in whatever work you choose, there will be a bit of the inventor/promoter. You should target yourself toward work that involves the big picture and bold concepts, rather than details and precise facts. You tend to pursue your interests by thinking less about the rules and procedures and more about the end goal. When you find that perfect relationship, job, or employer, you will be valued for the vision you provide as a catalyst for innovation and creative solutions.

ENTP
Contributions to an organization – you:
- Value achievement and are inspired to take yourself and others beyond stated goals;
- Are extremely flexible and versatile – you embrace ambiguity;
- Easily take the initiative and instigate change;
- Encourage and reward risk-taking;
- Delight in troubleshooting and conquering major problems;
- Generate creative ideas and are highly innovative;
- Think conceptually and are skilled in analysis;
- Brilliantly perceive market trends, future designs, and products;
- Find start-up projects exciting and routine processes boring.

Leadership style – you:
- Act as the visionary, persuading and inspiring others with enthusiasm and imagination;
- Are enlivened by crises, formulating theories, and constructing models;

- Prefer to ignore standard or traditional paths;
- Value ideas, energy, willpower, and ingenuity, consequently promoting and rewarding competence in your employees and colleagues;
- Prefer precision and are irritated by inefficiency and erronious information;
- Give credence to proficiency, not title or tenure.

Communication style preferences – you:
- Speak with passion and commitment, displaying wit and word play;
- Reply quickly with impromptu responses;
- Communicate in person, rather than in written reports;
- Are brief, succinct, and objective in written or spoken messages;
- Debate the pros and cons of various options;
- Discuss problems through unusual approaches and insights;
- Persuade others through cool, logical analysis and compelling examples.

Motivators and demotivators – you:
- Prefer the startup phase of a project, rather than the ongoing administration;
- Soar in environments where change, flexibility, and risk are present;
- Revel in designing plans and projects, building theoretical and conceptual models, and overcoming limitations;
- Appreciate opportunities to use your conceptual skills and creativity;
- Enjoy work that is not routine and where there is an absence of bureaucracy;
- Resist being overcontrolled and overmanaged.

As part of a group – you:
- Contribute lots of enthusiasm and energy;
- Dare the group to go beyond the status quo;
- Bring different viewpoints, clear ideas, inventive new insights, and information to the table;
- Provide analysis, solutions and identify opportunities;
- Irritate others at times by editing everything down to a theoretical model;
- Become frustrated with others who will not look at new prospects or who do not have a can-do attitude;
- Are sometimes irritated by coworkers who do not think abstractly and who make decisions emotionally.

Your learning style includes:
- A passion for learning where there is competition and a stimulating environment;
- Learning through participating in discussion and questioning others;
- Challenging teachers, facilitators, and classmates to be their best;
- Becoming easily bored once the problems or challenges are solved.

6 Description of the Individual Types

Suggested opportunities for growth – you should:
- Remember the importance of feelings – not everything is solved through logical reasoning;
- Pay more attention to details and project follow-through;
- Keep a balance between staying with present realities and looking to future possibilities;
- Learn how to use rules and regulations to advance your goals;
- Give more recognition and appreciation to others.

ENTJ – Extraverted/iNtuitive/Thinking/Judging

As an ENTJ your desire is to lead. Although other personality types may also be natural leaders, it has been said that an ENTJ cannot not lead. Your place is at the head of the crowd, marshaling everyone together and moving the group forward. You are rarely content to quietly stand back. On those occasions calling for you to follow, you do so, as long as you know that doing so will bring you closer to your goal.

You are keenly analytical. Analysis and objective criticism are second nature to you. As an ENTJ you often have a hard time understanding or appreciating appeals based on anything other than reasoning. You enjoy long-range planning and taking action. Your vision allows you to spot potential pitfalls far ahead, often beyond what is known and obvious. Your intellectual and curious mind thrives on new ideas, theories, and complex problems. Your organizational skills enable you to plan for all contingencies. The systematic style you use to map out the objectives enables you to arrive at your goals on schedule. Your penchant for quick, decisive action often leaves others behind. Problems invigorate you. You excel in positions that demand innovative solutions.

ENTJs are quickly disillusioned and unhappy when stifled or overcontrolled. You have little patience with uncertainty, timidity, emotionalism, inefficiency, or confusion. Making tough-minded decisions and taking hard actions do not scare you. ENTJs are comfortable with risk and unafraid of change. With such tenacity, work and home life easily intertwine. Direct in your dealings with people, you do not beat around the bush, but plunge ahead. You take as feedback what other personality types view as criticism. You tend to measure your own value by your accomplishments, but sometimes you set your personal standards for achievement impossibly high. ENTJs tend to live in the future much more than in the present and you tend to relate to people more on an "idea level" than on a personal one. Your creative intellect boldly challenges accepted theory.

ENTJ
Contributions to an organization – you:
- Readily and joyfully tackle confusion and inefficiency;
- Form commanding, thoughtful, and precise plans;
- Are highly strategic in choosing the direction of a project;
- Rarely take "no" for an answer;
- Delight in mental challenges and solving interesting problems;
- Generate results with lots of energy;
- Can be frank, decisive, and toughminded with people;
- Are unafraid of change;
- Are open to new ideas or strategies that allow moving forward quickly.

Leadership style – you:
- Generate energy and enthusiasm for work by leading directly;
- Objectively approach situations, goals, and the tasks at hand;

- Focus on results and accomplishing the long-term vision;
- Are logical, decisive, and unafraid of unpopular decisions and taking risks;
- Want independent and free-thinking colleagues and employees;
- Take pride in treating people well and utilizing resources to the maximum.

Communication style preferences – you:
- Speak with energy, excitement, and enthusiasm;
- Reply quickly with impromptu responses;
- Communicate in person, rather than in writing;
- Exhibit brevity, preciseness, succinctness, and analysis;
- Are direct and to the point, becoming impatient with extraneous details;
- Take pleasure in deliberating the pros and cons of various options;
- Persuade through objective reasoning, rather than emotions or values.

Motivators and demotivators – you:
- Enjoy situations requiring toughmindedness, strategy, and a long-term focus;
- Seek out opportunities to acquire more knowledge;
- Thrive when your hunger for problem solving is satisfied;
- Prefer situations where your vision is implemented;
- Seek efficient systems and people, or the opportunities to create such;
- Avoid situations where your freedom to marshal people, forces, and resources together is missing.

As part of a group – you:
- Bring total dedication to a project;
- Contribute by focusing on the long term, being goal-oriented, and delivering results;
- Are adept at finding flaws in proposed solutions;
- Sometimes appear too overpowering or controlling to others;
- Become irritated when others do not display your same level of commitment toward time;
- Are not interested in discussing an issue after closure has been reached;
- Are frustrated by anything that wastes time or resources and does not contribute to the goal.

Your learning style includes:
- A preference for learning to be a turn-on and a major way to move a career forward;
- Looking for action and variety in the classroom – you are interested in how information will affect the future;
- Learning best with an instructor who is well organized;
- Enjoying debate and verbal critiques of their work.

Suggested opportunities for growth – you should:
- Slow down once in a while – mistakes may occur when making decisions too quickly;
- Be sensitive to the needs and imperfections of people – you should consider others, give praise, and show appreciation;
- Let other people contribute leadership ideas;
- Remember to focus on the details, emotions, and values;
- Take into account all sides before making a decision.

ESFP – Extraverted/Sensing/Feeling/Perceiving

ESFPs approach life optimistically and are masters at living joyfully and entertaining others. You see the world as it is, approach it with curiosity, observe it well, embrace it openly, and adapt to whatever life may send your way. You are flexible, spontaneous, and practical. You are effective at communicating your good-natured realism to others. With your open, adaptive nature, you may earn the reputation of being a diplomat or mediator. You have a rare ability to suggest solutions and to encourage agreement and compromise.

ESFPs are keen observers and are endowed with a remarkable ability to integrate and deal effectively with enormous quantities of data – especially if the subject has something to do with the personal realm because their interests lie more in people than in things. You tend to greet the world with optimism, friendliness, warmth, compassion, and sympathy, wanting to ignore bad news and refusing to let gloomy people affect you. You are focused on people and are tactful and attentive to other people's needs and expectations. Essentially, you are a spontaneous individual – happy living life as it comes rather than walking the straight and narrow path defined by schedules, commitments, obligations, duties, rules, regulations, and the expectations of others. Typically, work and play are the same for you.

As an ESFP you are able to shift gears quickly, switching from one assignment to another and from one technique to the next. You thrive on action and are good in a crisis. You enjoy the challenge of handling unknown situations on a moment-to-moment basis, especially when the outcome is determined by your ability to apply your well-practiced problem-solving skills. The challenge for you is to achieve a balance between your jolly, easygoing nature and your ability to accomplish tangible results. Your style is one of grace, cleverness, and flair – you are a process-oriented person who appreciates risk-taking and adventure.

ESFP

Contributions to an organization – you:
- Bring optimism and a friendly, outgoing nature to work;
- Are spontaneous and flexible in adapting to situations;
- Seek challenge, excitement, and heroic opportunities;
- Have enormous talent for getting people to work together;
- Are a natural negotiator and trouble-shooter;
- Develop ingenious shortcuts to obstacles in the physical world;
- Enjoy hands-on work and lively, harmonious environments;
- Focus on generating practical, tangible results that benefit people;
- Like instigating change, if it solves a problem or dilemma.

Leadership style – you:
- Lead through promoting goodwill and teamwork;
- Focus more short-term than long-term and have a sense of immediacy;

- Are unafraid of change, creative solutions, and taking big risks;
- Usually leave implementation of plans to others;
- Effortlessly pull conflicting factions together by soliciting feedback and input from others;
- Pay attention to relationships first and completing tasks second.

Communication style preferences – you:
- Speak with energy and excitement;
- Reply quickly with impromptu responses;
- Communicate in person rather than in written reports;
- Use concrete and specific language;
- Use endless wit and abundant banter in communicating;
- Persuade others by emotionally presented, personal material;
- Communicate personal experiences to make points;
- Focus on the here and now.

Motivators and demotivators – you:
- Prefer work that is concrete, tangible, practical, and that benefits people;
- Want frequent opportunities to interact with people;
- Enjoy immediate action and crisis situations, especially where interpersonal conflict abounds;
- Enjoy work environments with choice, variety, and flexibility;
- Want harmonious and pleasant surroundings.

As a part of a group – you:
- Enthusiastically invite everyone to participate and join together;
- Clearly state tasks and objectives;
- Focus on accomplishing today's issues, problems, or projects;
- Build morale and an *esprit de corps*;
- Can irritate coworkers by overusing humor or clowning around too much;
- Become irritated by others who find fault and are cynical, gloomy, or contrary;
- Are annoyed by wasting time, lengthy boring discussions, and meetings.

Your learning style includes:
- Feeling there is much to gain when learning is fun and grounded in the present;
- Needing interaction, group projects, and hands-on experiences;
- Maintaining interest by understanding how material is useful, practical, and helpful in the here and now;
- Preferring caring instructors whom you can get to know well and who take a personal interest in you.

Suggested opportunities for growth – you should:
- Pay attention to balancing necessary tasks with socializing;
- Work toward prioritizing and completing tasks in a timely manner;

- Remember to value and work with all kinds of information;
- Realize that being overly optimistic and paying too much attention to the personal side of issues can lead to a disregard of logical facts;
- Pay more attention to the big picture and the future while balancing short-term concerns;
- Practice saying "no" to others to avoid becoming overloaded.

ESFJ – Extraverted/Sensing/Feeling/Judging

Outgoing and friendly by nature, ESFJs are greatly concerned with fostering harmony and cooperation. You are practical and conventional, sentimental and caring, all at once. Warm personal interactions and strokes of approval and appreciation keep you going in life. You are kind, unselfish, charitable, and naturally attracted to underdogs and those in need of a champion. Your sense of obligation is a driving force, pushing you to take on more and more responsibility for the benefit of others. Your desire to please others may be so strong that you may have a hard time taking criticism as anything put personal.

You tend to live strictly in the here and now with interests based in reality – experiences, things, and people. ESFJs are life's keen observers. You take note of everything you hear and hold an amazing number and variety of facts in your memory. You are not impressed by abstractions and theory. If asked to consider an idea, you prefer to see it first rendered into firm plans. Speculation and playing with theories do not interest you unless people are somehow at the heart of the matter. You tend to also be keenly aware of the feelings of others and the politics of business endeavors may cause you some anguish and concern. You need harmony to work happily and well. With your outgoing personality you prefer working with human companionship.

Communication in all forms comes easily to you. You are often an entertaining conversationalist and sympathetic, attentive listener. Being patient and conscientious, you make a concerted effort to stick to a job until it is finished, paying close attention to detail. When you join an organization, it is partly to satisfy the drive to belong to a group. You have probably found that you quickly accept responsibility in any group you join. ESFJs are the bedrock of any organization – the officers, the chairs of the working committees, those that get things done with an ultradependable style. ESFJs are the ones who establish, nurture, and maintain organizations.

ESFJ
Contributions to an organization – you:
- Are outgoing and sociable and you will maintain relationships;
- Are a hard worker who seeks responsibility and is always accountable;
- Are skilled at logistics and orchestrating resources to accomplish goals;
- Highly personalize the business process and outdo others in managing or selling concrete and tangible products;
- Carry out tasks efficiently and on time, with warmth and harmony;
- Perform with good organizational skills, leading to high productivity;
- Seek to minimize risk and prefer a conservative route;
- Are more comfortable dealing with facts and reality than with theories.

Leadership style – you:
- Tend to take charge when no one else does;
- Lead others through personal persuasion rather than through analytical reasoning;

- Show attention to others' needs, desires, and values, thereby building loyalty;
- Know when to focus on work and when to relax and socialize;
- Try to gauge the workload to avoid crises;
- Do not care for much change or circumventing stated policies/procedures.

Communication style preferences – you:
- Speak with energy and persuasiveness in concrete and specific terms;
- Reply quickly with impromptu responses;
- Talk in person, rather than communicating through written reports;
- Verbally map out the steps needed to accomplish a particular task;
- Present facts first, followed by practical applications;
- Focus on short-term current realities, rather than long-range future possibilities;
- Communicating personal experiences to make points;
- Persuade with emotionally presented, structured, and orderly material.

Motivators and demotivators – you:
- Operate best in stable and secure environments;
- Flourish in cooperative and harmonious environments;
- Are most productive when given clearly stated expectations;
- Prefer environments where the focus is on executing immediate details;
- Require enough time to complete projects timely, accurately, and orderly;
- Avoid situations where you cannot stay close to the project and people.

As a part of a group – you:
- Bring enthusiasm and organization to a group;
- Offer a systematic and practical outlook;
- Focus on time commitments, agendas, and practical methods;
- Acknowledge everyone's importance and contributions to the group;
- Become irritated by members who do not participate or take responsibility;
- Grow impatient with others who waste time or veer from the agenda during meetings.

Your learning style includes:
- Practical and pragmatic subjects with immediate applications for people;
- Working best on group projects or hands-on experiments that foster learning;
- A preference for structured learning systems requiring memorization, recall, and drills;
- Learning by experiencing a given topic or subject before reading it.

Suggested opportunities for growth – you should:
- Practice saying "no" to others to avoid becoming overloaded and burning out;

- Learn to give and receive feedback in a less personal manner;
- Be more flexible to changing decisions when new information arrives;
- Consider the suggestions of others for possible new ways of doing things;
- Remember to periodically take a look at the big picture instead of the tiny details.

ESTP – Extraverted/Sensing/Thinking/Perceiving

As an ESTP you see the world as it is, approach it with curiosity, observe it well, embrace it openly, and adapt to whatever life may send your way. You are flexible, spontaneous, and practical when it comes to any experience you can process with your five senses. ESTPs are people who must be free to experiment and experience life directly. You are happiest when you can live life today, doing things on impulse. You tend to do what needs to be done, moment by moment.

Work frequently becomes play and ESTPs are often great athletes, artists, craftsmen, and musicians. You thrive on action and are good in a crisis. You enjoy handling unknown situations, where the outcome is determined by your ability to apply your well-practiced, problem-solving skills. You have a zest for living and revel in the physical comforts of life – great food, nice clothes, good housing, and fun times. You place a high value on enjoying life, so whatever your financial prospects you will always find the means for recreation. It is no wonder that people genuinely like you and find your company to be a pleasure. Your challenge is to continually strive to balance your come-what-may open nature, with your less-developed organizing abilities.

ESTPs prefer to make decisions based on objectivity. In other words, you respect analysis and pay close attention to the external facts of any situation. You are a keen observer and deal effectively with enormous quantities of data. Many ESTPs have a lifelong fascination for machines, toys, instruments, tools, and other objects you can work with your hands. You are effective at communicating your good-natured realism to others. You also have a rare ability to suggest practical solutions along with encouraging agreement and compromise.

ESTP
Contributions to an organization – you:
- Provide optimism and a can-do attitude; work to remove obstacles;
- Are a master trouble-shooter;
- Are a skilled and vital negotiator;
- Strive for efficiency and results;
- Readily adapt to changing situations;
- Rely on firsthand experiences instead of theories;
- Are undaunted by and willingly accept risk;
- Provide grounded, blunt, and sober assessment of situations;
- Seek impactful solutions.

Leadership style – you:
- Motivate and inspire others;
- Enjoy solving immediate problems and making an impact;
- Dramatically and readily take charge in a crisis;
- Have the ability to blend differing views together and keep things moving forward;

- Structure environments for fun, flexibility, and motivating everyone to action;
- Expect leadership to be based upon performance, not position or length of employment.

Communication style preferences – you:
- Speak with energy, excitement, charm, wit, vitality, and dash;
- Reply quickly with impromptu responses;
- Talk in person rather than communicating with written reports;
- Skillfully mirror the language of others;
- Focus on current situations, not future concerns;
- Present information in concrete, realistic, no-nonsense terms;
- Persuade through common-sense logical analysis;
- Offer personal experiences to make points.

Motivators and demotivators – you:
- Need environments where opportunities and options abound;
- Value working in environments that call for action and quick decisions;
- Like associates who are equally hard working;
- Work best with a well-organized support staff;
- Relish challenge, thrive on solving problems, and opt for tangible payoffs;
- Avoid positions with diminishing freedom or where you feel controlled.

As part of a group – you:
- Provide clever solutions that yield practical results;
- Undertake the task of locating resources and removing obstacles;
- Easily incorporate the suggestions of others in a nonjudgmental, logical way;
- Establish objectives, routes, purpose, and benchmarks;
- May irritate team members by too-quick actions and spur-of-the-moment improvisations;
- Are irritated by team members who are reluctant to keep up with your pace;
- Become annoyed by people who are inflexible.

Your learning style includes:
- Excelling when learning is active and involves participation;
- Enjoying hands-on experiences and direct observations;
- Boredom with theorizing, long-range planning, focusing on concepts, and learning material that has little immediate relevance;
- Preferring instructors who are entertaining, fun, and who provide lots of activities; you do not hesitate to challenge instructors when they are too abstract.

Suggested opportunities for growth – you should:
- Set priorities and goals to avoid the appearance of being irresponsible or stressing others;
- Try to look beyond the quick fix and into the longer-term effects;
- Remember the feelings of others and try not to overlook them;
- Learn to value the benefits of theory, concepts, and abstractions;
- Be more tolerant of people who need inner contemplation and time before taking action.

ESTJ – Extraverted/Sensing/Thinking/Judging

You are a natural organizer of your environment. You use your reasoning ability to take charge of as much of your life as possible. You are most comfortable when a situation allows you to plan ahead, get the facts, set goals, lay out a timetable, and organize the resources. Those objectives usually concern people, objects, and situations rather than theories and ideas. ESTJs trust information that is rooted in the real world. You have patience with familiar tasks, familiar skills, and familiar routine. You work steadily toward your goals with greater accuracy than other types. You enjoy the predictability of a well-laid-out life.

ESTJs are natural managers who pour their energy into the job. You have little sympathy for ineffective or inefficient work. You have a clear-cut view of what it means to do a job well. You are open and straightforward about your views, preferences, prejudices, and decisions. You prefer clear-cut choices and display intolerance toward ambiguous situations. When considering an idea, you prefer to see firm plans – complete with facts and figures – before you invest your time and energy. But unless you take the time to slow down and attend to other people's points of view, you may judge too quickly.

ESTJs like a harmonious, orderly, routine home life that emphasizes traditional values. You value your possessions. Given a choice, you will spend your money on useful furnishings and major pieces that will see many years of service. You are unsettled by waste and conspicuous consumption. You have a distinct sense of obligation and responsibility, a driving force that pushes you to take on more and more tasks for the benefit of others. Because of your organizing abilities and realistic observations, people with this personality type often represent an important component within civic and social groups. Friends appreciate the ESTJ's ability to look at any situation in a practical, no-nonsense way. ESTJs are product-oriented people who set, appreciate, and value high standards.

ESTJ

contributions to an organization – you:
- Complete tasks accurately, on time, with all details in place;
- Gets results and are a natural sales person;
- Masterfully create efficient systems;
- Are action-oriented and do not hesitate to be tough-minded;
- Are practical and realistic, moving step-by-step toward goals;
- Handle problems directly and decisively;
- Organize and structure processes and people;
- Like accomplishment and actual, physical, practical applications;
- See little usefulness in change, particularly if things are working fine.

Leadership style – you:
- Are a born administrator of resources, people, and projects;
- Prefer to concentrate on the work, not the people conducting the work, but offer appreciation to those who earn it by producing;

6 Description of the Individual Types 71

- Are direct and resolute in getting to core issues;
- Use time-tested, established methods to achieve short-term results;
- Are conservative toward change, set high standards, and stick to them;
- Believe authority is gained over time by producing positive results.

Communication style preferences – you:
- Speak with energy and forcefulness;
- Reply quickly with impromptu responses;
- Communicate in person, not by writing reports;
- Use brevity, succinctness, objectivity, and mental exactness;
- Use concrete and specific, rather than abstract and theoretical speech;
- Present facts, followed by practical applications;
- Are convinced, and convince others, by orderly, objective reasoning.

Motivators and demotivators – you:
- Prefer a stable, secure, predictable, and consistent environment;
- Seek opportunities to work with people who follow through;
- Prefer surroundings where you can interact with people;
- Work best in an atmosphere that provides a sense of belonging;
- Need to know that your efforts have tangible and practical payoffs;
- Avoid situations where you do not have responsibility or cannot maintain control.

As a part of a group – you:
- Are a natural team player;
- Bring a driving force for planning and accomplishment;
- Challenge others to live up to your high standards of excellence;
- Are concerned with present realities, not future concerns;
- Conduct business with a no-nonsense and direct manner;
- Become frustrated by meetings that are not focused or fail to follow clear agendas;
- Do not appreciate actions that waste time or stray away from the task at hand.

Your learning style includes:
- Preference for structured lessons that have a purpose, with no deviations in the schedule;
- Learning best with hands-on, concrete activities – drills and memorization tasks;
- Preferring fact-oriented teaching and finding little use for impractical concepts;
- Expecting instructors to be fair, consistent, and to evenly apply the rules.

Suggested opportunities for growth – you should:
- Watch your tendency to be blunt and try to consider the needs, desires, and feelings of others;

- Periodically modify your expectations of others to keep people motivated;
- Learn the art of giving positive feedback;
- Be open to new ways of doing things – listen to others' ideas, alternatives, and information;
- Pay closer attention to the "big picture" to balance short-term goals.

INFP – Introverted/iNtuitive/Feeling/Perceiving

As an INFP you are capable of immense sensitivity and have an enormous emotional capacity, which you closely guard. You have to know people well before you display warmth, let down your guard, and extend your trust. Relationships are a crucial focus for you. You seek to understand others deeply and to have that understanding reciprocated with loving acceptance.

INFPs value inner processes over external signs. You guide your actions and attitudes by a strong internal sense of values that is independent of the judgments of others. You have a powerful sense of faithfulness, duty and commitment to the people and causes that attract you. You take your obligations seriously, enforced by your own sense of morality. Genuineness and sincerity are what matter to INFPs. You know instinctively how to reach people and how to communicate your concerns. More than any other personality style, you are able to express emotion and to move people through your communications.

Functioning in a sea of people may be exhausting and draining for you. But, living a life of isolation would be unimaginable. INFPs prefer a quiet working environment and, despite your attraction for human companionship, will often find that you work best when alone. You will find your greatest comfort through interacting with others, closely, intimately, in small, cooperative groups or one-on-one. INFPs trust their inner vision and are willing to act at an instinctual level. You look toward the future. Creativity is your hallmark. You see whatever you do as an extension of who you are and, therefore, you are driven to do your best at any task you undertake.

Harmony is essential for you. You seek to promote peace and cooperation. INFPs are masters of the well-placed compliment and the encouraging pat on the back. INFPs also have no trouble shifting gears from one task or assignment to another. You are at your best in a job you truly believe in. Whatever field you choose, your INFP style will be marked by sincere enthusiasm, born of your deep commitment to your calling.

INFP
Contributions to an organization – you:
- Are creative and see the big picture;
- Prefer working on a few projects that have deep meaning;
- Enjoy cooperative environments and work for the development of people;
- Are conceptually oriented, always pushing for your values;
- Are unafraid of change and comfortable with ambiguity;
- Like solitude and concentrate intensely on your projects;
- Are idea-oriented, always seeking new possibilities;
- Are more project-driven than deadline-driven;
- Desire freedom from structure to respond quickly to situations.

Leadership style – you:
- Are subtle, indirect, gentle, passionate, and inclusive;
- Affirm individual contributions and promote group undertakings;

- Accomplish results in your own way;
- Enjoy challenges and finding solutions – and are unafraid of taking risks;
- Pay careful attention to the people involved during crisis situations.

Communication style preferences – you:
- Keep your energy and excitement inside yourself;
- Reflect before replying and waiting to be drawn out;
- Speak with individuals instead of large groups;
- Use speech that is more global and metaphoric than detail-oriented;
- Speak of ideals, values, and the big picture;
- Persuade and are persuaded by emotionally presented, personal material;
- Communicate personal experiences to make points.

Motivators and demotivators – you:
- Enjoy fun projects, but not loud, noisy environments;
- Desire freedom from structure and rules and like timelines and schedules that are flexible;
- Function best when working one-on-one or in small groups;
- Seek work that is meaningful and contributes to the betterment of people;
- Appreciate personal acknowledgment;
- Dislike discord, mindless routine, and work filled with detailed data.

As a part of a group – you:
- Bring quiet good humor to the group and orchestrate unity and harmony;
- Provide provocative ideas, future possibilities, and a big-picture viewpoint;
- Are gentle, friendly, listen intently to others, and offer encouragement;
- Inspire and move people to go beyond the status quo;
- Provide vision and a focus on ideals and values;
- Like to work with people who are open to new ideas, possibilities, and different opinions;
- Become irritated by overly serious team members.

Your learning style includes:
- Preferring flexible environments where you can use imagination and creativity;
- Learning best from lectures and written work, rather than rote methods;
- Enjoyment of abstractions and the world of ideas;
- Preferring trainers who are personally interested in you.

Suggested opportunities for growth – you should:
- Learn to determine if visions and plans are practical and workable;
- Try to focus more on action and "doing" instead of reflection and contemplation;
- Be careful with your time to avoid burnout; your highly empathic nature can lead to being neglectful of your personal needs;

- Practice depersonalizing critical feedback and learn to give constructive criticism to others;
- Remember to share ideas, dreams, and visions so others can help you realize those dreams.

INFJ – Introverted/iNtuitive/Feeling/Judging

You are an imaginative, inspired, tenacious, creative, and inward-looking individuals. Outside obstacles and expectations mean less to them than the high personal standards you set for yourself. INFJs make value-based decisions easily and your friends and associates tend to perceive you as self-confident and individualistic.

You live in a world of ideas. You focus on the possible, develop plans to bring your ideas into practice and pour all of your energy into achieving your goals. You often see problems well before they arise and decide in advance what to do in case of difficulties. You trust your intuition and are not afraid to act on an instinctual level. Your ability to make value judgments on the basis of intangible data often baffles others, but your experiences usually validate your insights. You know instinctively how to reach people and communicate with clarity. You, better than any other personality type, can express emotion and move people with your written communication.

Genuineness and sincerity are what matter to you. You do not casually reveal your inner self to others. INFJs invest their time, energy, and affection in only a few people, measuring friendships by depth and longevity, rather than by breadth or number. You seek to understand others deeply and to have that understanding reciprocated. Although you cherish the companionship of people, you prefer a quiet working environment, often finding that you work best when alone. To perform at your peak, you require a harmonious working environment. You are a true perfectionist when it comes to the quality of your work and creativity is your hallmark. It is critical for an INFJ to stop for a moment and pay close attention to your own personal needs so that the flower of your creativity can reach full bloom.

INFJ
contributions to an organization – you:
- Are quietly forceful, personable, and genuinely concerned for others;
- See possibilities and relationships missed by most others;
- Have single-minded concentration and the ability to follow through;
- Offer insight about future opportunities;
- Like tackling complex issues involving people and material;
- Focus on building harmony and work toward the common good;
- Generate innovative solutions to complex problems;
- Bring creativity and a future orientation to an organization;
- Trust and pursue your own unique and creative inner vision, even if it means taking risks.

Leadership style – you:
- Become an advocate for others and their talents when leading;
- Inspire others to follow through your enthusiasm and faith;
- Place intense attention and persistence on bringing your inspirations into reality;

6 Description of the Individual Types

- Prefer planning in advance and covering all contingencies to avoid crises;
- Are willing to be a pioneer, venturing forth into uncharted territories;
- Courageously challenge confirmed experts or popularly accepted beliefs.

Communication style preferences – you:
- Keep your energy and excitement contained;
- Need time to reflect before replying and waiting to be drawn out;
- Speak with individuals rather than large groups;
- Prefer written reports over talking in person;
- Use language that is global and colorful, instead of precise and plain;
- Give new insights and use unusual approaches;
- Persuade and are persuaded by emotionally presented, personal material;
- Communicate personal experiences to make points.

Motivators and demotivators – you:
- Function best within a quiet and orderly environment;
- Need caring and harmonious surroundings;
- Appreciate positive feedback about your unique contributions;
- Seek opportunities to learn, grow, and solve problems;
- Prefer the freedom to express and carry out your ideas;
- Avoid situations where you cannot be creative and innovative.

As a part of a group – you:
- Encourage harmony and get everyone to contribute;
- Provide big-picture overviews and in-depth synopses;
- Bring creative and clear-sighted perceptions and visions to the table;
- Masterfully synthesize people, resources, goals, and visions;
- Become irritated by team members who show little caring for others;
- Irritate others by stubbornly clinging to an idea;
- Dislike pessimistic members and those who fail to contribute.

Your learning style includes:
- Valuing lifelong learning by interacting with others or through reading and writing;
- Preferring tools and materials that are organized;
- Enjoying future-oriented concepts, theories, abstractions, and ideas;
- Avoiding dictatorial educational settings, as well as black-and-white thinking.

Suggested opportunities for growth – you should:
- Practice being more objective, realistic, and open to current facts;
- Learn when to cut your losses if visions do not pan out;
- Practice speaking up about ideas – be more assertive;
- Not take criticism or conflict too personally;
- Remember to pay attention to personal needs to prevent burnout.

INTP – Introverted/iNtuitive/Thinking/Perceiving

Like great theoreticians with analytical genius, INTPs have the ability to pursue a goal single-mindedly, avoiding distractions and sidestepping obstacles. Originality, insight, and creativity are hallmarks for INTPs. You have great insight, intellectual curiosity, speed in understanding, ingenuity, and a wealth of ideas for dealing with problems. Absorbed by the inner world of thoughts and ideas, you use your rational abilities in an adept, objective, and impersonal manner. Your friends and associates are likely to describe you as subtle, imaginative, ingenious, and a bit shy.

Your strength lies in your ability to thoroughly work out the fundamental principles of a system, an operation, or a problem. As an INTP you tend to happily lose yourself in your world of thoughts. Moving from one intuitive understanding to another is effortless for you. Before you communicate your thoughts, you will always first make sure you have them clearly organized internally. As a result, you may sometimes be seen as reserved and withdrawn. Because of your desire to correctly express your thoughts and concepts, conversations can quickly turn into articulating the exact truth about even the tiniest pieces of the entire puzzle.

You deeply appreciate learning and fascinated by the very concept of intelligence. Always setting high standards, you maintain a mental list of things you should learn, accomplish, and master. You are such a perfectionist that, at times, you don't always realize you have passed the point when it was "good enough." You prefer a quiet working environment and can easily work alone. Working long hours without a break is not bothersome to you. You tend to always be scanning the horizon for new or overlooked possibilities in any situation. This characteristic allows you to be an explorer and a visionary. In the main, you appreciate intelligence, continually seek to increase your knowledge, and see possibilities beyond what is present, known, or obvious.

INTP
Contributions to an organization – you:
- Seek to continually acquire new knowledge and competencies;
- Are flexible, unstructured, and see beyond rules and procedures;
- Are a strategist and visionary;
- Use systematic intellectual precision and expertise in problem solving;
- Enjoy the world of ideas, analysis, and designing complex systems;
- Have strongly defined interests and enjoy working on an intellectual level;
- Are a reserved, quiet, and deeply reflective high achiever;
- Become utterly absorbed in seeking answers to your major interests.

Leadership style – you:
- Usually prefer to work autonomously while solving complex problems;
- Prefer intellectual rather than emotional interaction, relating to others through expertise;

- Establish an agenda and stay focused on the long term;
- Present options for groups to make majority or consensus decisions;
- Meet crises creatively but do not take unnecessary risks;
- Believe in competence, not title and tenure.

Communication style preferences – you:
- Keep your energy and excitement contained inside yourself;
- Reflect on your response before replying and need to be drawn out;
- Speak with individuals rather than large groups;
- Prefer written reports over talking in person or in meetings;
- Comment briefly and succinctly without repetition and redundancy;
- Give highly complex and abstract presentations;
- Persuade and are persuaded by thoughtful, rational analysis;
- Use thorough, objective reasoning rather than personal examples.

Motivators and demotivators – you:
- Need to achieve, acquire new knowledge, and become more competent;
- Prefer nonemotional, objective environments where justice and accuracy prevail;
- Excel when not hampered by rules, procedures, and day-to-day routine;
- Like peace and quiet and time to reflect alone;
- Prefer opportunities to research, analyze, and design future projects;
- Become irritated with errors, redundancies, and inefficiencies.

As part of a group – you:
- Tend to be reserved and contribute to group goals by working alone;
- Solve problems and identify underlying issues;
- Offer impartial observations and perceptions, using logic and reason to support decisions;
- Naturally become the expert resource on issues;
- Can irritate others by being too intellectual and reducing everything to logical statements;
- Become frustrated when a lack of vision, direction, and commitment is present;
- Are disturbed by waste and interruptions.

Your learning style includes:
- Adherence to a life-long learning philosophy that is deeply reflective;
- Concentrating on concepts, abstract theories, identification of working principles and categorization, and boredom with rote drill and the memorization of details;
- Focusing on the broad picture and delving deeply into the subject;
- Not hesitating to challenge instructors and facilitators.

Suggested opportunities for growth – you should:
- Try to notice and comment on things people are doing right;
- Pay greater attention to follow-through and taking action;
- Practice letting go of minor inconsistencies that keep projects hanging indefinitely;
- Increase communication with others so they can understand your thinking;
- Ask others for feedback; with your perfectionist tendencies, you are your own worst critic.

INTJ – Introverted/iNtuitive/Thinking/Judging

Imaginative, inspired, tenacious, creative, and driven are all words that describe an INTJ. You live in a world of pure ideas, concepts, and associations so unique to your mind that not many others can share your vision. You are self-confident and individualistic, and typically do not need permission or understanding from the world to believe in yourself.

You enjoy roaming from one project to the next, focusing your particular competence on the next invention or reorganization. You approach life as an inventor, innovator, organizer, and reviser. You tend to be good at filtering out extraneous information so that you can focus on the critical issues to formulate plans, settle conflicts, and wrap up deals with a minimum of delay. But you may also restrict the flow of information by allowing discussion of only what you consider to be "the essentials."

You have an inner drive for performance and continually strive for self-improvement. You probably set high standards for yourself, creating mental lists of things you should learn, accomplish, and master. INTJs often will find the time to tackle the most difficult problem and unravel the most complicated situation. You are inclined to make decisions on an impersonal and objective basis. You may be aware that such impersonal behavior negatively affects values-based people, but you also recognize the importance of clear thought.

Your mode of thought in any profession will basically be scientific in nature, where you can apply your models to real projects. Overall, as an INTJ you tend to be a person who appreciates intelligence and continually seeks to increase your knowledge.

INTJ
Contributions to an organization – you:
- Are a master of ideas and systems and of designing and building new models;
- Excel at analysis and strategy development;
- Have faith in your own inner vision, your willpower, and ability to move mountains;
- Are emphatically determined to accomplish goals and master new skills;
- Enjoy working where there is freedom to envision and design plans;
- Design and implement plans for the most efficient and effective use of existing resources;
- Are brilliantly and boldly innovative in thought and action;
- Prefer to work alone and rarely consult with others;
- Are unafraid of change and complex problems.

Leadership style – you:
- Are forceful and decisive in leadership roles, focusing more on tasks than relationships;
- Provide focus to define, determine, and accomplish a stated purpose;

- Move quickly in a crisis once all the pieces of the puzzle are in place;
- Are unafraid to completely overhaul an entire organization if necessary;
- Believe competence is important, not assigned titles or length of employment.

Communication style preferences – you:
- Communicate only those elements deemed essential and not stating the obvious;
- Reflect before replying and need to be drawn out;
- Speak with individuals rather than large groups;
- Prefer written reports over talking in person;
- Use brevity, succinctness, objectivity, and mental exactness;
- Persuade others through clear thinking, logic, and debate;
- Are persuaded through cool, logical analysis and unusual insights.

Motivators and demotivators – you:
- Like to plan, design, and implement models, systems, and efficient long-range strategies;
- Enjoy working with other self-reliant individuals and require autonomy;
- Like structure and order, would rather not attend too many meetings, and need plenty of private time for introspection;
- Find the ambiguous exciting and enjoy striving for clarity;
- Avoid environments governed by bureaucracy, protocol, and paperwork.

As part of a group – you:
- Contribute if your participation will get the job done;
- Provide strategy, vision, the bigger picture, and new perspectives;
- Systematically schedule and complete tasks on time;
- Analyze the alternatives and offer new perspectives, long-term strategy, and vision;
- Irritate others by sometimes being single-minded in completing a task or project;
- Become irritated by others who don't show respect for your ideas or questions;
- Are impatient with team members who are slow to grasp information.

Their learning style includes:
- Being an analytic, independent, and resourceful learner who is bored by routine;
- Enjoying the time and liberty to become totally absorbed in a topic of interest;
- Learning by developing and organizing models that explain how something works;
- Being challenged, particularly by instructors or facilitators you respect.

Suggested opportunities for growth – you should:
- Notice things people are doing correctly before pointing to their mistakes;
- Be more aware of the motivations, attitudes, emotions, and needs of others;
- Strive for greater flexibility and openness;
- Learn to bring others into projects, ideas, and designs; practice delegating;
- Learn to master the more concrete and routine details, even though you find more fun and enjoyment in the theoretical and abstract world.

ISFP – Introverted/Sensing/Feeling/Perceiving

You are cheerful, lighthearted, warm, and sensitive, and your deeply held values are sometimes hidden from the view of others. Your focus on your personal values and take the task of clarifying what is most important to you very seriously. For others to see you only as carefree and lively is to overlook your depth and complexity.

You are highly empathic. You gather an abundance of information about others and seek to understand what it means and how you can use it to be of help to them. You are often exceptionally accurate in your assessments of others. You generally have an optimistic, here-and-now personality that is strongly oriented toward practicality. Your spontaneity and sense of humor contributes to your reputation as being a person who knows how to play. You are often happiest when you can live life today – unencumbered by boring or demanding routines. Activity and action make you most happy. ISFPs love the real world: nature, tangibles, gadgets, tools, and things you can work on with your hands. You like doing anything that expresses who you are, in a direct, physical way.

ISFPs prefer communication that is clear, understandable, direct, and precise. You are a hands-on problem-solver, in a warm, sympathetic, people-oriented way. You are highly sensitive to other people's feelings and needs and have a deep desire to please. You praise the accomplishments of others, lend a sympathetic ear to their problems, and try to avoid being the bearer of bad news. Yet, you are courageous and bold when tackling problems or tasks that require an immediate, practical solution. ISFPs tend to be mentally active at all times, but have a unique ability to balance reflection and action. You immediately grasp what is necessary in a situation and then take action without getting lost in evaluating all the other possible options. Because you are calm in a crisis and able to easily and quietly sort through tangled information with flair, it appears that you find a solution without much effort. But that is simply one of your many talents.

ISFP
contributions to an organization – you:
- Are optimistic in attitude and outlook;
- Are unafraid of risk and change, particularly if you instigate it;
- Focus on the human side of work and the well being of others;
- Use personal loyalty, along with gentle persuasion, to motivate others;
- Avoid convoluted problems and believe that talk is cheap – "show me results";
- Are at your best when responding to a crisis;
- Are tactical by nature; like challenge, variety, and nonrepetitious work;
- Desire to make an impact with your solutions and results;
- Bring craftsmanship and aesthetics to your work;
- Love to overcome obstacles;
- Are reflective and practical, solving immediate and concrete problems;
- Bring people and tasks together in a cooperative manner.

6 Description of the Individual Types

Leadership style – you:
- Rise to any occasion and readily adapt;
- Seek the most expedient solution to a problem;
- Like to work independently and call the shots, and admire the creative initiative of others;
- Believe in superior performance, not rank or tenure.

Communication style preferences – you:
- Keep energy, excitement, and enthusiasm inside;
- Reflect before replying and wait to be drawn out;
- Prefer to speak with individuals rather than large groups;
- Receive information in short summary form;
- Use concrete and specific language – action speaks louder than words;
- Communicate personal experience to make points;
- Persuade and are persuaded by emotionally presented, personal material;
- Focus communication with others on the here and now.

Motivators and demotivators – you:
- Enjoy activities where you can become totally absorbed;
- Like flexible schedules and nonroutine work – you welcome surprises;
- Enjoy variety, challenge, excitement, and opportunities to solve problems;
- Prefer hands-on projects that need action and concrete, specific results;
- Seek freedom from rules, procedures, regulations, hierarchies, and strict lines of authority;
- Avoid working with "doom and gloom" people.

As a part of a group – you:
- Are dedicated to accomplishing whatever needs to be done;
- Bring a quiet humor to the team;
- Generate here-and-now ideas, which others can then pursue;
- Bring a strong dose of common sense to projects and solutions;
- May annoy others with your extreme sensitivity;
- Have difficulty with a group that won't collaborate or cooperate;
- Can become annoyed with team members who are intolerant of the ideas and contributions of others, or who come late and are disrespectful to others.

Your learning style includes:
- Liking subjects that are relevant, practical, applicable, and focus on people;
- A preference for learning situations where you have flexibility, freedom, and spontaneity;
- Learning best through hands-on experience;
- Thriving in an environment with caring instructors and lots of encouragement.

Suggested opportunities for growth – you should:
- Develop the ability to give critical feedback and be more objective;
- Not take criticism so personally and instead turn it into useful feedback for personal growth;
- Practice meeting deadlines and following a schedule;
- Learn to balance present-day realities with the big picture;
- Remember to pay attention to personal needs to prevent burnout;
- Learn to speak up so your contributions and accomplishments will be recognized.

ISFJ – Introverted/Sensing/Feeling/Judging

Hardworking, thorough, and responsible, you are the Rock of Gibraltar. People can lean on you for assistance with good cause. You provide stability and trust. You will never undertake any enterprise or go into any relationship impulsively or frivolously, nor will you forsake it for any but the soundest and most well documented reasons. You are a permanent resident of the here and now, continually comparing today's data with what you collected yesterday and all the yesterdays before.

You have the outlook of a traditionalist who believes in structure, responsibility, and rules for living. You are happiest when living a well-defined life. You want to know where things are and when events will happen. You appreciate a predictable environment and are patient and comfortable with routine. You have a realistic view of what you can and cannot accomplish.

You expect a great deal from yourself and judge your behavior by tough standards. Setting your goals high, it is rare that you really satisfy your own scrutiny of how you should perform. You have a strong need to feel needed by others. You quickly accept responsibility in any group you join. The bedrock of any organization – officers, committee chairs, the doers – is made up of ISFJs with their supremely dependable personalities. You establish, nurture, and maintain an organization. You need peace, quiet, and few interruptions to work most comfortably. Whatever the task, you spend time reflecting before acting and are in your element when you find work that gives you ample time for contemplation. You are precise, seldom making errors of fact. Others, with less attention to detail, strike you as unreliable. You will be happiest in an unambiguous position, with well-understood expectations, regular hours, and predictable activities. With your respect for procedures and policies, you can function happily and productively at almost any level of an institutional hierarchy.

ISFJ
contributions to an organization – you:
- Are practical, dependable, and conscientious with strong follow-through;
- Like tackling projects with here-and-now benefits for people;
- Desire privacy, quiet, and few interruptions;
- Are intent on the details;
- Support, assist, and empower members of the organization;
- Have low-key, long-lasting, and disciplined energy;
- Are a "doer" that likes to get things accomplished;
- Respect and follow systems, procedures, and lines of authority;
- Provide an atmosphere of belonging and permanence and avoid risk-taking.

Leadership style – you:
- Exhibit an open, encouraging, and supportive leadership style;
- Focus on the people involved in conducting business, yet stay on track with the tasks;

- Are a stickler for details and will see what others might miss;
- Plan in order to avoid crises;
- Look out for the organizational needs of your followers;
- Adhere to traditional hierarchies and lines of authority.

Communication style preferences – you:
- Provide practical and pragmatic discussion with a focus on values;
- Prefer time for reflection so you can reply in a diplomatic manner;
- Speak with individuals instead of large groups;
- Prefer written reports rather than talking in person;
- Speak in language that is concrete, factual, and specific;
- Discuss immediate, practical approaches;
- Persuade and are persuaded by emotionally presented, personal material;
- Use personal experiences to make points.

Motivators and demotivators – you:
- Seek a stable and predictable environment, preferring little or no change;
- Prefer schedules and completion dates that allow you to achieve practical results;
- Appreciate the opportunity to work alone, yet still have some interaction with people;
- Like to work toward realistic, tangible goals, doing one thing at a time;
- Appreciate personal acknowledgment for your hard work;
- Avoid projects that do not require your logistic and quantitative skills.

As part of a group – you:
- Provide clear directions, organizational skills, practicality, and concrete, factual input;
- Try to promote the viewpoints, ideas, and suggestions of others;
- Keep the team on track by paying attention to detail and accuracy;
- May annoy team members with a singular focus on present-time results;
- Become frustrated with too much focus on possibilities while ignoring factual data;
- May frustrate others when you do not always speak up for their ideas;
- Are annoyed by those who do not follow a schedule and who go off on tangents.

Your learning style includes:
- Preferring learning as part of a team or group;
- Working best through drills and memorization where results can be measured;
- Dealing with problems that are clear-cut and concrete while avoiding theoretical concepts;
- Working to please instructors by providing them with exactly what is requested.

Suggested opportunities for growth – you should:
- Develop greater assertiveness and comfort in taking the lead;
- Learn to share ideas and accomplishments more often;
- Learn to become more comfortable dealing directly with conflict;
- Try being more open to change and new ways of doing things;
- Balance short-term practical vision with future possibilities.

ISTP – Introverted/Sensing/Thinking/Perceiving

As an ISTP you use highly developed rational abilities to keenly observe and objectively analyze situations. You usually concentrate on the way life actually works, not why it works the way it does. You use your thought processes to help you get things done. You approach new ideas or situations in a very basic manner, asking, "What does it do?" "How does it do it?" and "Can I use it?"

When you are absorbed in figuring out how to do something or make something work, you carefully avoid distractions and obstacles that dilute your focus. You can easily become engulfed in any one of your favorite activities. ISTPs take pride and interest in whatever they do and are good at precise work, seldom making errors of fact. You also have the habit of saying nothing when everything is all right, but pointing out problems immediately as they arise. Your friends are likely to describe you as somewhat shy, persevering, practical, factual, and solidly grounded in the present.

You must also be free to experiment and experience life directly. You are happiest when you can live life today, doing things on impulse. ISTPs thrive on action and are good in a crisis. You enjoy dealing – moment by moment – with situations where the outcome is determined by your ability to apply your well-practiced problem-solving skills. Often the ISTP holds a lifelong fascination with machines, instruments, devices, tools, and other such objects. You can easily create or work with your hands. However, you may find that communicating freely and easily does not come as effortlessly as it does for others. The data person in you emerges and you may find that you are attempting to cover every last detail in an effort to be precise and clearly understood. You are in your element when you find ample time for contemplation. You have the ability to attain success in your pursuits because of your highly practical nature and your focus on achieving results.

Contributions to an organization – you:
- Enjoy the risks that accompany change;
- Are optimistic and cheerful when tackling issues with a group;
- Are a concrete, linear thinker and doer;
- Are highly adept in mechanical and technical arenas;
- Enjoy solving concrete problems, preferably independent of others;
- Easily marshal resources and energy to solve immediate problems;
- Excel when results are immediate and suffer when the process is too boring;
- Are project, action, and short-term results oriented;
- Focus on solving the problem, regardless on the amount of time it takes to produce results.

Leadership style – you:
- Set an example, lead through action, and are pragmatic and unobtrusive;
- Seek high-impact performances and look for expedient solutions;
- Troubleshoot and remain calm during crises, calculate risks, and look before leaping;

6 Description of the Individual Types

- Respond quickly when trouble is on the horizon;
- Work best with flexible employees;
- Foster independence in your workers but are not attentive to social niceties.

Communication style preferences – you:
- Talk in concrete, realistic, no-nonsense terms, with sharp-witted humor;
- Reflect before replying briefly and need to be drawn out for further information;
- Speak to the point with individuals instead of groups;
- Provide short synopses in verbal or written reports;
- Use objectivity and specific images in all forms of communication;
- Relate personal experiences to make points;
- Persuade and are persuaded through common sense and logical analysis.

Motivators and demotivators – you:
- Like opportunities to work alone and focus on the task, not on people;
- Appreciate pleasing surroundings and optimistic coworkers;
- Seek opportunities to be creative, take risks, and solve crisis situations;
- Need freedom to work autonomously;
- Solve specific and concrete problems that are difficult and unusual;
- Avoid routine and mundane details.

As part of a group – you:
- Are the storehouse for facts, figures, details, and different points of view;
- Organize tasks efficiently with your analytical skills;
- Persevere regardless of obstacles;
- Focus on solving current and immediate problems with flair;
- Are greatly annoyed by contrary behavior and illogical people;
- Are disdainful of meetings without a practical purpose;
- Do not enjoy constant teamwork – you want action and can become impatient with delays.

Your learning style includes:
- Increasing your practical knowledge and skills through independent learning events;
- Learning by doing, firsthand observation and one-to-one hands-on activities;
- Studying how something works, what its technical properties are, and what uses it has;
- Preferring instructors who have real-life experience.

Suggested opportunities for growth – you should:
- Practice opening up and sharing verbally so others are not surprised by your actions;

- Develop the habit of setting goals, planning, and sticking to a schedule;
- Practice developing greater sensitivity to the needs of others;
- Carefully think about the long-term implications of present-day actions;
- Focus on seeing results from current projects before jumping onto the next bandwagon.

ISTJ – Introverted/Sensing/Thinking/Judging

The ISTJ is a "no-nonsense" individual who is exceedingly dependable. You are the most practical of all the personality types, skillfully saving data, money, and materials. Accuracy is paramount. You absorb information and remember details with thoroughness. People can lean on you with good cause. You never undertake any enterprise or relationship impulsively or frivolously, nor will you forsake it for any but the soundest and most well documented of reasons.

You are likely to be attracted to business, commerce, or technical arenas where you will excel with your ability to meet a particular need. You can easily shift gears and change course if you have the necessary data to support such decisions. Too much illogical change can make you uneasy. You avoid any more change than is absolutely necessary. Preferring the predictable, you want to know where things are and when events will happen. You value an orderly home life that emphasizes traditional values. You tend to take care of your possessions (office equipment, household furnishings, etc.) and can become unsettled by waste and conspicuous consumption. You expect a great deal from yourself and use tough standards to judge your own behavior.

The ISTJ's view of life is so strongly linked to the work ethic that you feel play must be earned by having first worked diligently. ISTJs establish and maintain organizations. You will probably find that once you have become a member of an organization, you quickly accept positions of responsibility.

You need time alone to work most comfortably. Putting in long hours on a project without a break does not bother you. You take pride in your contributions to a project and develop great interest in all facets of whatever job you tackle. Overall, your valuable, systematic approach to problem solving and perseverance in finding solutions lends stability to any cause with which you are associated.

ISTJ

Contributions to an organization – you:
- Work steadily and efficiently to accomplish stated goals;
- Are strongly oriented toward detail and achieving results;
- Are hard working, thorough, orderly, and prefer uninterrupted privacy;
- Bring a strong dose of reality, objectivity, and measurable results to an organization;
- Have a no-nonsense attitude when working to meet objectives;
- Act quickly and accurately when a decision or action is necessary;
- Honor commitments and work best with timelines, deadlines, and structure.

Leadership style – you:
- Delegate authority once the situation, with all available facts and figures, is under control;
- Pay attention to the immediate needs of the organization;

- Are a reliable leader who organizes tasks, staff, and operating procedures;
- Prefer to avoid crises by planning well in advance;
- Set standards and expect others to follow through, rewarding those who follow the rules.

Communication style preferences – you:
- Speak in a calm and composed manner with rare displays of private reactions;
- Reflect before replying and wait to be asked for further information;
- Prefer to speak with individuals instead of large groups;
- Prefer written reports rather than talking in person;
- Use brevity, succinctness, objectivity, and mental exactness;
- Present facts in a direct, pragmatic manner, followed by practical application;
- Persuade and are persuaded by others through cool, logical analysis;
- Communicate personal experience only to backup points already made with other data.

Motivators and demotivators – you:
- Enjoy structure, order, consistency, a steady pace, and few interruptions;
- Excel in situations calling for perseverance and tenacity;
- Appreciate rewards for your concrete accomplishments;
- Are diligent when involved with tangible projects, concrete products, and short-range results;
- Enjoy logistical work and moving the organization forward;
- Avoid environments that are chaotic and unfocused.

As a part of a group – you:
- Work best with established rules and procedures;
- Concentrate on meeting deadlines, timelines, and priorities;
- Run meetings like clockwork – efficient, focused, and impersonal;
- Use dependable common sense in tackling projects and assigning tasks;
- Are concerned with the tangible tasks immediately at hand;
- Sometimes hold back expressing your viewpoint until it is too late;
- Are irritated by too much talking, irrelevant chatter, unrelated interruptions, and lack of follow-through by others.

Their learning style includes:
- Learning best by utilizing memorization and drills, and having time to reflect;
- Finding practical and useful applications for the subject you are studying;
- Highly valuing organization, accuracy, and precision in materials and directions.

Suggested opportunities for growth – you should:
- Practice being more openminded to innovation, change, and new ways of doing things;
- Remember to consider the impact of values when making decisions;
- Avoid becoming so lost in details that the larger picture or subtle interactions are ignored;
- Try to be more flexible when applying the rules;
- Practice occasionally saying "no" to added responsibilities to prevent burnout.

7 Stress

Stress impacts personality – strengthening preferred functions and/or exposing our inferior function. Stress and tension are triggered by the environment, which impacts personality.

Personality impacts stress – different personalities respond to different stressors and to stressors in different ways. Some personalities cower under particular stressors, whereas other personalities seem to deal quite well with the stressor.

Stress can be very productive (eustress) or can paralyze energies (distress). Personality-type dynamics explain patterns that might disturb the individual, and offer strategies to handle stress at the same time.

Stress is an issue each individual has to deal with.

Jane was a huge fan of Paul Newman. In the early 1990s, Paul Newman was still racing cars. He was scheduled to race at Brainerd International Raceway in northern Minnesota. Upon hearing that Newman would be only 3 hours away, Jane cajoled her husband into driving from St. Paul to Brainerd in hopes of seeing Paul Newman. Leaving Friday afternoon and arriving in Brainerd that evening they started to look for Newman – with no luck. All day Saturday they looked as well (not going to the races), and Sunday morning they looked as well – no luck. Midafternoon on Sunday Jane's husband indicated that it was time to get back to St. Paul. As they were driving south out of town on Highway 218, there was a small ice cream shop. Jane suggested: "I would like some ice cream," so they pulled in. Her husband was not hungry and indicated that he would wait in the car. Jane could grab some ice cream and they would be on their way.

Upon entering the ice cream shop – there sat Paul Newman – right by the door! Jane was very excited, nervously went up to the counter and ordered her ice cream. She drew a deep breath and said to herself, "I am a mature woman, I can handle this" and as she turned, Newman looked up and smiled. Jane blushed and ran out to the car. "He is in there. He is in there" she blurted. "Did you get his autograph?" her husband asked. "No, but I saw him and he smiled at me! He's great!" Jane exclaimed. "Where is your ice cream"? her husband asked. "Oh, I must have left in on the counter" Jane sighed. "I'll go in and get it". As Jane walked back into the ice cream shop, she looked up and down the counter – no ice cream. Just as she turned, Newman looked up and said: "It is in your purse!"

Now that is a funny story. But according to type it was typical. Jane had a preference for iNtuition and Feeling. She was an NF big-picture, enthusiastic, emotive type. When under mild or controlled stress, she would become even more big-picture, enthusiastic, and emotive. In this state Jane would use her preferred functions more dramatically. Specifics and details are clearly not important and often lost. Ice cream in a purse did not even register in the reality of being in the presence of Paul Newman.

Generally, when subjected to mild stress our preferred functions are spurred into action. We give it our best in such situations. This is supported by current research from neurobiology.[7] We know that each type has a set of preferences. Thus, each type will likely respond to mild stress in similar patterns. That is, we could expect that other NFs would likely respond in a big-picture subjective overview, whereas an ST would respond to mild stress with accentuated detailed objectivity (they would never plop ice cream in a purse without being aware of it).

7.1 Definition of Stress

We all live within "comfort zones" – a dynamic balance of tension. For example, my most preferred blood pressure may be 110 / 80. Yours may be 100 / 75. We each have many unique tensions that we prefer that are most healthy for us – blood pressure, body temperature, heart rates, and the like. The same is true with our psychic attitudes and functions: Healthy harmonies are established. What is most comfortable, productive, and efficient for our personal system is the tension that we call our "comfort zone." A more technical and operational definition for stress may be helpful here:

Anything that moves us out or our comfort zone is considered stress. Stress is environmental or internal perturbations that challenge or

disrupt our regulatory mechanisms. From a systems perspective, stress disrupts the system. It can disrupt the system by inducing either negative or positive feedback.

Stress is experienced by an individual if their physical and/or mental constitution is not yet fit enough to meet the environmental demands. Whenever the dynamic equilibrium of a system is challenged (not ready to change) stress is experienced. The dynamic equilibrium (comfort zone) is based on the current physical and mental constitution of the individual.

Stress disrupts our comfort zone. The stress response is the way in which we are adjusted to the requirements of an ever-changing world. The stress response is the physiological and psychological reaction to changes or challenges from the environment. Stress is the outcome or response to our individual unique perception of an event or situation.

Jane was pulled out of here comfort zone when she was in the presence of Paul Newman. Had Jane's husband gone in to purchase the ice cream, he may not have been stressed at all. Stress is very personal. Each of us has and defines our own comfort zone.

Systems (and a person – you – can be considered a system) always exhibit a dynamic tension: A comfort zone. However, when pulled out of (or pushed inward from) that comfort zone, we experience stress.

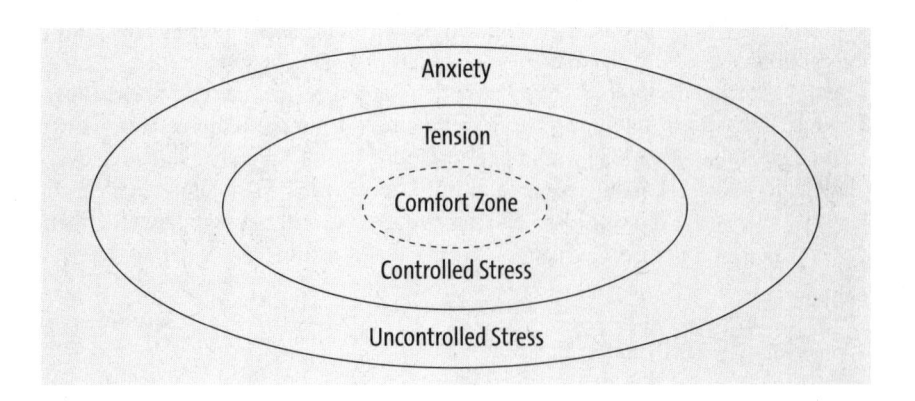

When we are mildly pulled or pushed out of our comfort zone and sense some tension, we experience controlled stress. When pulled or pushed beyond tension (way out of our comfort zone), we may experience uncontrolled stress.

7.2 Controlled Stress

Controlled stress or mild stress occurs when a situation or an event is perceived to be controllable. It occurs when we believe that we can change our behavior to cope with the stress. If you can cope or adapt to a stressor insofar as to render it negligible, this would be considered controlled stress. In these instances, preferred functions are relied upon to manage the situation.

Repeated exposure to one and the same controllable stressor results in the successive facilitation of certain coping strategies, and therefore a behavioral specialization – we get better at what we were good at. Actually, in these times your brain adjusts its response (but does not change the structure) and thus your behavior is altered. This means that the next time you are faced with the same stressor you are either not stressed by the situation – because of the adaptation – or you have developed psychological coping strategies. Nice. That is to say that if Jane would repeatedly meet Paul Newman in an ice cream shop she would eventually be much calmer – her comfort zone would expand to include such celebrities.

7.3 Uncontrolled Stress

Uncontrolled stress occurs when an event or experience is perceived to be beyond control. In such instances our response systems become a trigger for the adaptive reorganization of the associative brain. The brain and the psyche go deep, mining all that the conscious and subconscious have to offer. When exposed to uncontrolled stress, the brain physiologically changes (the structure of the brain is actually changed).[8] For example, a person living in London (or Berlin) during World War II may cease hearing bombs because their brain has rewired itself to shut out the sound of bombs. Or, a battered woman will cease to think about the fact that getting hit in the face is violent. There are not many funny stories here.

> Another example:
> *I was looking forward to meeting friends in Paris – which was wonderful. Having a preference for NF, I had numerous visions of enjoyment. Then, at an intersection very near my home, I heard a high-pitched squeal. The next thing I realized, my car was pushed off the road. A motor bike had hit my front wheel, dislodging any steering capability and the biker was lying under my car. I started to reason: I should back up the car so the biker could get up again. I turned the ignition key: No noise. The motor would not start; lucky for the motorcyclist. I got out of the car. A truck driver on the other side waved across and shouted: "I am a witness, the biker did not stop at the stop sign. You are not guilty." As I walked across, I felt calm, the picture of guilty–not guilty was wiped out in my brain. I just realized I had broken into the biker's life, because I was a part of the system. I felt guilt.*

But what happened inside my head? Calm, no high emotions. Reason (my inferior T) prevailed in my NF world. A paradigm shift of "justice" had occurred.

I had a completely different image than before. That is uncontrolled stress in the anxiety zone: It provokes a paradigm shift. I had clearly entered the anxiety zone, a different picture, or paradigm, had been created. The synapses in my head went crazy. They calmed down when the police officer said that the biker was not seriously injured and when I called a nearby friend who drove me back home. And Paris offered a nice comfort zone after this angst-filled event.

Psychologically, according to type, in times of uncontrolled stress the inferior function takes over. We are beside ourselves[9] – in the grip of something that is not normal for us, certainly not preferred, and not comfortable – but perhaps somewhat typical. Different inferior functions illicit different types of behavior. These are uncomfortable moments and often difficult times. However, the rewired brain may also allow us to "see things with new eyes," to "breathe new air," to "feel a warmer sun" and "to understand at a deeper level." The changed brain structure provides a new paradigm – a new world view. This is not always bad.

An individual's brain is rewired after experiencing uncontrolled stress. This rewiring may help to develop positive behavior or in other instances may lead an individual toward depression or other pathologies. The result of uncontrolled stress can be good, but it can produce results that we deem as bad.

7.4 Summary

For practical reasons we differentiate three areas. The first area we call a "comfort zone." We all have comfort zones – and we need those to relax and to allow us to be who we are. Imagine an island vacation: Sunshine, waves, and a nice breeze, day after day on the beach. How does it affect the brain? It rests. It reposes on standby. Now we must be vigilant. If the brain dulls and retires, you will be pushed out of your comfort zone. You don't have to be 60 years old to retire. A 20-year-old person can be in the state of retirement – no creativity, dull routines, operating on standby. You need stimulation to maintain the dynamic tension necessary for your comfort zone. On the other hand, you don't need a tsunami to stimulate you into action. This would be pulling you out of your comfort zone in the other direction. Be vigilant. Know the limits of your comfort zone. Know the tension that you can withstand in the second area and celebrate the fact that your preferences are being strengthened. And brace yourself for the anxiety and uncontrolled stress of the third area and be ready to learn from that experience.

When you know your harmonies of tension and your personality type you can make the necessary adjustments to live more often in your comfort zone. The following pages outline typical responses to controlled and uncontrolled stress. We also offer suggestions to reduce controlled stress and lessons that can be learned from uncontrolled stress.

Typology sharpens personal awareness and offers controls for handling stress.

7.5 Stress by Type

ISTJ

The preferred functions of the ISTJ are dominant introverted sensing and secondary extraverted thinking. This ST combination becomes more exaggerated and more pronounced under controlled stress.

When experiencing controlled stress – you:
- Heighten attention to tasks and details;
- Become impatient with others who do not see the relevant facts or who deny them;
- May hesitate in making decisions, holding out a bit longer before drawing conclusions;
- Issue terse, cold, hard statements;
- Increase resistance to change;
- Believe that the stressful condition may last forever – it now is a matter of fact.

When the ISTJ falls into the grip of the inferior function (extraverted iNtuition) the behaviors change dramatically.

When experiencing uncontrolled stress – you:
- Become obsessed with the big picture;
- Come up with unrealistic and offbeat expectations;
- Explore many options at once;
- Express impatience at the lack of more opportunities;
- Compulsively look for more possibilities;
- Become uncharacteristically loud.

Suggestions to reduce controlled stress – as an ISTJ you should:
- Engage in more physical exercise;
- Change your environment (go on short vacation, rearrange furniture, etc.);
- Remind yourself that paying close attention to facts and details does pay off;
- List your assets (capabilities, talents, strengths, etc.).

ISTJ lessons from uncontrolled stress:
- Unknown and/or unfamiliar events occur – that is a fact.
- Past experience plays a large and relevant role in the big picture.
- You can be flexible with details, facts, and responsibilities.
- When you are at your best, you will be taken seriously and not judged as irrational.

ISFJ

The preferred functions of the ISFJ are dominant introverted sensing and secondary extraverted feeling. When experiencing controlled stress this pair of functions (**SF**) take charge of the ISFJ behaviors.

When experiencing controlled stress – you:
- Become overly nurturing or sweet;
- Focus on each detail for each need of each individual around you;
- May hesitate a bit longer before making critical decisions;
- Seek to maintain the status quo at all costs;
- Believe that every specific ill is your fault;
- Believe that this life is tough and it will probably never get any better.

The ISFJ will be under the influence of extraverted iNtuition when in the grip of the inferior function. It could be said that the ISFJ loses control in a "big" way.

When experiencing uncontrolled stress – you:
- Scream that the world is "going to hell in a hand basket";
- Compulsively look for new relationships;
- Become obsessed with all the suffering in the world, realizing that nothing can be done;
- Become uncharacteristically verbose;
- Lose your calm demeanor;
- Escape into a world of dreams.

Suggestions to reduce controlled stress – as an ISFJ you should:
- Engage in more physical exercise (yoga, running, etc.);
- Focus on what you are doing in a charitable activity (giving money, volunteering, etc.);
- Rearrange your physical environment (even if only for a short time);
- Ask for help with overpowering details.

ISFJ lessons from uncontrolled stress:
- Hitting bottom and playing out fears and anxieties will not last forever.
- Being more accepting of yourself will result in new viewpoints of yourself and others.
- Knowing what is real and concrete are important factors in complex relationships.
- Understand that you can be accepted regardless of temporary outbursts.

INFJ

Dominant introverted iNtuition and secondary extraverted feeling are the preferred functions for the INFJ. This **NF** pair guides behavior in a more dramatic and pronounced way when stress in part of the context.

When experiencing controlled stress – you:
- Quietly worry about meeting the expectations of everyone else;
- Constantly expect obstacles and problems to plague you;
- Become more self-critical, restless, and frustrated;
- Internalize global issues (world hunger, overpopulation, war);
- Determine to become the most caring and considerate person on earth;
- Mind-map all of the possibilities to control your stress.

The INFJ submits to an extraverted sensing as the inferior function. The extraverted S demands attention and completely embarrasses the INFJ.

When experiencing uncontrolled stress – you:
- Become obsessed with the specific needs of others and loudly challenge others to assist;
- Lose sight of the big picture and are very short-sighted;
- Worry about getting each task accomplished today;
- May become mentally fatigued and not think clearly;
- Indulge in sensual pleasures (overeating, exercising, sleeping, binge shopping, etc.);
- Are worried and alarmed by present immediate tasks.

Suggestions to reduce controlled stress – as an INFJ you should:
- Focus on a relationship with a close friend;
- Know that you are being listened to without others offering advice, insight, or judgment;
- Relax by taking a walk in nature, seeing a movie, or reading poetry;
- Pare down your schedule and carve out time for solitude.

INFJ lessons from uncontrolled stress:
- Ambitious visions can be reconstructed into doable chunks.
- Creating more sensual experiences can have value.
- Doing today prepares you for living tomorrow.
- Getting specific, concrete tasks done today will build a better future.

INTJ

Dominant introverted iNtuition and secondary extraverted thinking dictate the behavior for the INTJ. This function pair (**NT**) becomes increasingly rigid and more dominant when experiencing stressful conditions.

When experiencing controlled stress – you:
- Become controlling and directive;
- Map out the possible alternatives and scheme how to manipulate the outcomes;
- Are silently intense and driven;
- Limit communication to only essential and critical exchanges;
- Generate more options and alternatives than are necessary;
- Hesitate until completely ready to share ideas and become intolerant of intrusions or interruptions.

When in the grip of the inferior function (extraverted sensing in the case of the INTJ), behaviors change dramatically, but not for the better for the individual or for those around them.

When experiencing uncontrolled stress – you:
- Lose sight of your global perspective and become concerned with the immediate;
- Become obsessed with facts and details and make many factual errors and mistakes;
- Obsessively clean the house or car, rearrange furniture, or organize cabinets or closets;
- Vocally express displeasure at the lack of sufficient detail;
- Micromanage immediate tasks;
- Attack all specific data that challenges your competence.

Suggestions to reduce controlled stress – as an INTJ you should:
- Relax and get a good night's sleep;
- Focus on your thinking abilities to structure a problem and create a plan for resolution;
- Cancel activities that are not part of the solution and create time for solitude;
- Exercise, read, or take a long walk.

INTJ lessons from uncontrolled stress:
- Working with unfamiliar details can increase your competence.
- Volumes of new data can be organized and elegantly sophisticated.
- Interruptions to your daily routine or tasks can assist in your well-being.
- Gentle humor can be productive.

7 Stress 105

ISTP

The ISTP exhibits preferred functions of secondary extraverted sensing and dominant introverted thinking. This **ST** preference demands objectivity, analysis, and silent control that are pronounced when under stress.

When experiencing controlled stress – you:
- Intensely focus on the precise moment and the immediate facts;
- Express anxiety or annoyance with very subtle body language, such as a raised eyebrow;
- Become increasingly isolated from the world;
- May be obstinate in applying the correct logic;
- Obsessively try to solve the immediate problem;
- Approach unsolvable problems as doable and must solve them before moving on.

The inferior function for the ISTP is extraverted feeling. The expression of this unexpected and misunderstood subjective logic is quite out of character for the ISTP.

When experiencing uncontrolled stress – you:
- Express strong feelings (emotions);
- Become agitated, vague, distractible, and disorganized;
- Take criticism personally and easily overreact to the innocent remarks of others;
- Lose your ability to focus on each element of the issue;
- React swiftly (and loudly) in anger, sadness, or frustration;
- Feel unloved and unlovable.

Suggestions to reduce controlled stress – as an ISTP you should:
- Engage in challenging but mostly physical activities like hiking or rock climbing;
- Find time alone to read, play solitaire, or do activities with repetitive handling;
- Delegate others to run errands and deal with the outside world;
- Get a "reality check" from a knowledgeable person (expert).

ISTP lessons from uncontrolled stress:
- Accept that life and people are sometimes just not objective.
- Accept vulnerability and realize, therefore, that you are not always objective.
- Realize that there is some comfort and safety in expressing the depth of feeling.
- Recognize the difference between knowing your values and feeling the values.

INTP

The INTP finds the preferred functions in secondary extraverted iNtuition and the dominant introverted thinking. These functions guide the NT in deliberate, objective analysis.

When experiencing controlled stress – you:
- Become deliberate, exacting, and dogmatic;
- Clearly align all variables in controlling ways;
- Apply a clear and precise logic to all comments or issues;
- Know what is right and demand that the right thing be done;
- Isolate yourself from the world;
- Obsessively try to include everything into the big picture.

When the inferior function (extraverted F) comes into play, the INTP exhibits uncharacteristically emotional and unexpected behaviors.

When experiencing uncontrolled stress – you:
- Lose your problem-solving abilities and self-confidence;
- Are unable to express ideas articulately, ramble, and are clearly agitated;
- Become socially awkward;
- React swiftly (and loudly) in anger, sadness, or frustration;
- Feel discounted, criticized, trivialized, and not listened to;
- Feel controlled or "boxed in."

Suggestions to reduce controlled stress – as an INTP you should:
- Spend time alone, reading, doing crossword puzzles, or taking quiet walks;
- Focus on a new idea, insight, or perspective that has relevance to the situation;
- Quietly talk about your thoughts and perceptions with a nonjudgmental, trusted person;
- Reduce the amount of noise and/or distractions.

INTP lessons from uncontrolled stress:
- Accept the fact that at times things are just plain subjective.
- Expressing the depth of feeling is the normal course of events in personal development.
- Recognize that to be vulnerable is not disastrous.
- Letting go is not a form of control.

ISFP

The ISFP finds guidance from the preferred extraverted secondary sensing and dominant introverted feeling. The generally mild and gentle ISFP, under stress, becomes hypersensitive to remarks of others and their own expectations.

When experiencing controlled stress – you:
- Feel strongly that you have not lived up to other people's expectations;
- Fear loss or separation of significant relationships;
- May create upsets where before there were none;
- Become hypersensitive;
- See all the negative and destructive elements in the world;
- Are increasingly frustrated by having to work alone to make the world a better place.

The grip of the inferior function (extraverted T) dramatically changes the behaviors of the ISFP. In such instances, the ISFP exhibits behaviors that are cold, crass, and often loud.

When experiencing uncontrolled stress – you:
- Become intolerant and inflexible, and lose compassion;
- Demand concrete evidence of progress or decisions being made;
- Do not want to be discounted because of lack of expertise or data;
- Call for more objectivity in difficult times;
- Silence others with sharp criticism;
- Obsess over the lack of discipline and analysis.

Suggestions to reduce controlled stress – as an ISFP you should:
- Let events and attitudes run out of energy in their own time;
- Find time and space to reflect on what is important to you;
- Start a craft project using familiar and well-practiced skills;
- Find a trusted friend to validate your feelings.

ISFP lessons from uncontrolled stress:
- Understand and accept your need for power and objectivity.
- Objectivity supports your values and enhances understanding.
- You do not always have to live up to the expectations of others.
- Removing yourself from the situation can bring comfort and satisfaction.

INFP

The preferred functions for the INFP are secondary extraverted iNtuition and dominant introverted feeling. The INFP, when experiencing stress, often exhibits a negativity that permeates most situations.

When experiencing controlled stress – you:
- Feel inadequate and overwhelmed and may be unable to complete even the simplest task;
- Surround yourself with an atmosphere of negativity and feel a lack of authenticity;
- Are easily filled with feelings of self-doubt;
- Can engage in destructive judgments and fantasies about anything or anyone convenient;
- Feel compelled to take action to correct real or imagined mistakes;
- Sees all problems as connected.

The inferior function for the INFP is extraverted T. There is a dramatic shift from the normally accepting, understanding, and open behaviors. The extraverted T demands, is aggressive, and consumes the INFP.

When experiencing uncontrolled stress – you:
- See things as "black or white" opposing scenarios;
- Become blunt and direct when talking with others;
- Demand competence from those around you;
- May ignore others' contributions if the suggestions do not fit into the "correct" analysis;
- Can nitpick, relentlessly emphasizing order, accuracy, analysis, and legalistic logic;
- Attempt to control situations via objectivity and removing yourself.

Suggestions to reduce controlled stress – as an INFP you should:
- Let events and problems dissipate on their own volition;
- Meditate and find time and space to reflect and reconfirm basic values;
- Create a new approach to an existing project, or pursue an intriguing insight;
- Engage in a solitary activity, take a long walk, cook a fine meal for yourself, etc.

INFP lessons from uncontrolled stress:
- Tempered idealism and expressions of objectivity do have their place.
- Exerting your full authority is necessary for authenticity.
- Values are reinforced and supported by principles and objective thought.
- Strategic plans do have their place.

ESTP

The preferred functions of the ESTP are dominant extraverted sensing and secondary introverted thinking. The effervescent ESTP, under stress, becomes more pragmatic, begins to doubt his- or herself, and pays special attention to detail.

When experiencing controlled stress – you:
- Lose your good-hearted sense of humor;
- Begin to doubt your abilities to clearly calculate the processes;
- Fear that others will see you as incapable and not correct;
- View any change as threatening or negative;
- Become precise, exacting, and concise;
- Obsess over details and are not willing to come to a conclusion or decision too quickly

The ESTP in the grip of the inferior function (introverted iNtuition) suddenly takes a quiet turn into a big and open world that is frightening and overwhelming.

When experiencing uncontrolled stress – you:
- Withdraw from the world and feel lonesome, gloomy, sad, and quiet;
- Become overwhelmed and overburdened by a multitude of competing possibilities;
- Allow your thinking to become confused and somewhat illogical due to numerous options;
- Retreat in quiet reflection and contemplate the negative state of the world;
- Resist conforming to any schedule, structure, or request;
- Respond with ambiguous answers to questions and requests.

Suggestions to reduce controlled stress – as an ESTP you should:
- Devise rational and sensible contingency plans;
- Convene a group (friends) to discuss your situation and provide objective feedback;
- Engage in vigorous physical activities with others (team sports);
- Monitor more closely your eating habits and food intake.

ESTP lessons from uncontrolled stress:
- Ambiguity is not all that bad.
- The unknown future can be approached and dealt with.
- Trusting your intuition is almost fun at times.
- Quietly exploring fantasies is helpful to place reality in the appropriate context.

ESFP

Extraverted sensing is the dominant function for the ESFP which is supported by the secondary introverted feeling. The good nature of the ESFP is accentuated in the serving nature when under stress, and then things turn pessimistic.

When experiencing controlled stress – you:
- Become pessimistic and worried and take feedback from others too personally;
- May experience fears about losing or damaging close relationships;
- Overcompensate while caring for others – doing more than necessary or appropriate;
- Look to help many others;
- Allow the process of "serving" to become much more important than the result or outcome;
- Fear that you may not be doing enough specific acts of kindness.

The ESFP, when in the grip of the inferior function (introverted iNtuition) falls prey to all of the ills of the world in a big way and feels isolated in the process.

When experiencing uncontrolled stress – you:
- Lose your easygoing, agreeable nature;
- May allow feelings of isolation to produce significant anxiety;
- Interpret random and innocent events as ominous signs about the future;
- Feel uncomfortable by having too many duties, obligations, and responsibilities;
- Struggle with issues of authenticity and self-esteem;
- Feel compelled to take on the responsibilities of all humanity.

Suggestions to reduce controlled stress – as an ESFP you should:
- Convene a group of friends to validate yourself and your position and/or situation;
- Establish contingency plans consistent with your values;
- Play with friends in active physical activities, dance, group games, etc.;
- Focus on activities connected to making a positive difference for people.

ESFP lessons from uncontrolled stress:
- The unknown future can be very positive for all involved.
- Ambiguity can be tolerated and enhance your values.
- Quiet reflection on possibilities and options does produce good.
- Change can be consistent with what you believe.

ENFP

The ENFP continues to try to take in all of the world when under stress. The preferred functions of dominant extraverted iNtuition and secondary introverted feeling work overtime in attempts to accommodate everything.

When experiencing controlled stress – you:
- Overextend and overcommit – and feel overextended and overcommitted;
- Become emotionally sensitive, believing no one appreciates or cares about you;
- Repeatedly try to fit all competing factions into a harmonious whole;
- Feel guilty for not having done more;
- May neglect yourself in the concern for the larger community;
- Try all possible options.

When in the grip of the inferior function (introverted sensing) the ENFP makes a dramatic withdrawal from virtually everything and takes a rather negative view of the world.

When experiencing uncontrolled stress – you:
- Lose enthusiasm, optimism, and energy for life – it is no longer fun;
- Withdraw and become depressed, sad, and despondent;
- Escalate small issues into major problems;
- Take on a narrow focus and project the results into a gloomy future;
- Feel guilty for not living up to specific expectations of others;
- Become hypersensitive about personal comments.

Suggestions to reduce controlled stress – as an ENFP you should:
- Converse with others in a judgment-free context;
- Exercise, sleep more, eat better foods, get a massage;
- Connect with others who provide warmth, kindness, and approval;
- Explore possibilities without setting a priority order or making a decision.

ENFP lessons from uncontrolled stress:
- Taking care of yourself physically improves life quality.
- Quiet time spent on details is enriching, and develops better organizational skills.
- A regular, more disciplined approach can be fulfilling.
- Focus on a particular issue can provide a "light at the end of the tunnel."

ENTP

The ENTP displays a clear dominant extraverted iNtuitive and secondary thinking function preference. This **NT** preference pair pulls the ENTP to ever-widening horizons. When stressed, these grasps for the bigger picture are more dramatic.

When experiencing controlled stress – you:
- Focus on tasks and may neglect food or rest, thereby creating exhaustion or illness;
- Become overly critical, believing no one understands you;
- Become exceedingly analytical and dogmatic;
- Demand that all options be linked and tied together in a complete whole;
- Require that all options be explored, no stones left unturned, and all data be reviewed;
- Become more agitated, louder, rapid, and demanding in your speech.

The inferior function of the ENTP is introverted sensing. When in the grip of the inferior function, the ENTP forgoes the comprehensive endeavors and focuses attention on what is immediately before them.

When experiencing uncontrolled stress – you:
- Turn very irritable, rigid, or crabby;
- Lose verbal skills, such that talking with others becomes difficult;
- Place high priority on immediate, specific, concrete tasks;
- Become literal and insensitive (focusing exclusively on task);
- Take narrowly focused data and erroneously project results with few choices or options;
- Intensely focus on immediate data and how it can be improved (micromanage).

Suggestions to reduce controlled stress – as an ENTP you should:
- Converse with others in an objective context and not push for closure or decisions;
- Analyze the events and determine the order of things;
- Connect with others who provide neutral perspectives;
- Explore possibilities and probabilities without setting a priority or making a decision.

ENTP lessons from uncontrolled stress:
- Details do have relevance to larger problems.
- Quiet time spent on details is productive and develops clearer organizational skills.
- You can accept assistance with details.
- Focusing on a detail can allow you to see the whole (as in holograms and fractals).

7 Stress

ESTJ

The ESTJ is driven by the preferences of the secondary introverted sensing and the dominant extraverted thinking. This combination is clearly working to manage and control the external environment.

When experiencing controlled stress – you:
- Try to hide your inner turmoil and stay in control;
- Become cold and harsh and are seen as uncaring;
- Make clear, crisp, succinct arguments;
- Hold rigidly to an isolated fact, example, or principle;
- Intensely (loudly) argue for action at this precise moment in time;
- May become fatigued and find it difficult to maintain your logical thinking.

The dramatic behavioral shift for the ESTJ occurs when the inferior function (introverted feeling) seizes control.

When experiencing uncontrolled stress – you:
- Have difficulty making decisions and taking effective action;
- May lose your natural self-confidence and self-esteem;
- Withdraw into silence, becoming moody and depressed;
- Can feel isolated, unappreciated, and alone;
- May not share your inner turmoil with others;
- Can lash out at others in seemingly emotional outbursts.

Suggestions to reduce controlled stress – as an ESTJ you should:
- Take a vacation with friends;
- Rehearse arguments and important positions;
- Accept silent support and objective feedback;
- Get a good night's sleep, eat better, and engage in physical activities with friends.

ESTJ lessons from uncontrolled stress:
- Sharing the depth of feeling with trusted people works wonders.
- You can now appreciate their limitations.
- Others can be quite subjective (and so can you).
- Close relationships are necessary for your well-being.

ENTJ

The ENTJ generally exhibits a strong personality. When under stress the secondary introverted iNtuition and the dominant extraverted thinking become even more pronounced.

When experiencing controlled stress – you:
- Become louder and more argumentative;
- Hold to dogmatic positions;
- Try to control all situations and hide inner turmoil;
- Demand responses to all requests;
- Delegate more and more responsibilities;
- Call for clearer accountability from all others.

The introverted feeling function is the inferior for the ENTJ.

When experiencing uncontrolled stress – you:
- Feel that prized principles have been ignored, compromised, or transgressed;
- Lose your cool, objective, take-charge tough-mindedness;
- Can feel isolated and emotional when needing to make a decision;
- May overreact to even mild comments made by others;
- Obsess over a subjective "wrong" decision;
- Feel that others are out to get you.

Suggestions to reduce controlled stress – as an ENTJ you should:
- Explore (play with) hypotheses and possibilities that move you beyond your stressors;
- Create interesting and clear arguments and clarify important positions;
- Talk to friends who provide clear analysis and objective feedback;
- Clarify the things under your control.

ENTJ lessons from uncontrolled stress:
- Sharing the depth of feeling with trusted people works wonders.
- You, too, have limitations and subjective feelings that can lead to deeper understanding.
- Close relationships can be productive and may even be necessary for your well-being.
- There is a source of power that you have not yet tapped.

ESFJ

The ESFJ is guided by preference for introverted sensing and the extraverted dominant feeling functions. Stress diminishes the usual open, friendly, and accepting ESFJ to less accepting and more critical behaviors.

When experiencing controlled stress – you:
- Become hypersensitive to emotions yet find them hard to accurately express;
- Can become depressed, feeling vulnerable and unworthy;
- Tend to feel numb inside, seeing only a bleak future;
- Tend to become intensely self-critical;
- Can easily find fault with others;
- Complain of too many demands being placed upon you.

Introverted thinking is the inferior function for the ESFJ. When in the grip of the inferior function, the ESFJ experiences a dramatic shift from the value-driven behaviors to quiet objective analysis.

When experiencing uncontrolled stress – you:
- Turn optimism and enthusiasm into seclusion, inertia, and dejection;
- Grow even more organized and bound to plans, turning into a perfectionist;
- Tend to be intensely self-critical;
- Become obsessed in searching for the "real" truth;
- Use complicated and convoluted analyses in pursuing the truth;
- Will try to "think" yourself out of a problem, but get stuck in faulty logic.

Suggestions to reduce controlled stress – as an ESFJ you should:
- Engage in strenuous physical activity, be outside, run;
- Share (sound-off) your deepest feelings and anxieties with trusted friends;
- Surround yourself with those who support you and provide specific nurturing feedback;
- Get involved in a focused, detailed, and methodical project or hobby (journaling, cooking).

ESFJ lessons from uncontrolled stress:
- Your concerns are heard and taken seriously.
- You now have a greater appreciation for your objective and analytical abilities and limits.
- You can face distress with greater neutrality.
- Life sometimes intrudes on your desired peace and harmony.

ENFJ

The function preferences for the ENFJ are introverted iNtuition and dominant extraverted feeling. This NF combination turns on itself when under stress.

When experiencing controlled stress – you:
- Feel distrusted, undervalued, or unable to get issues resolved;
- Feel you have to conform to too many popular views that you find distasteful;
- Tend to turn more self-critical;
- Become intensely focused on authenticity and being true to yourself;
- May feel vulnerable and unworthy;
- Verbally lash out at all of the demands being placed upon you.

The inferior function for the ENFJ is introverted thinking. When in the grip of the inferior function, the ENFJ isolates him- or herself and attempts an objective approach to getting out of trouble.

When experiencing uncontrolled stress – you:
- Become isolated and see yourself as misunderstood and unclear;
- Withdraw into silence, brooding over issues of truth and justice;
- Use complicated and convoluted analyses in pursuing truth and justice;
- Will try to "think" yourself out of a problem, but get stuck in faulty logic;
- Silently scheme to make all things right;
- Become rigid and aggressive in dealing with others.

Suggestions to reduce controlled stress – as an ENFJ you should:
- Find a support group you can talk with about your frustrations;
- Allow yourself to share your deepest feelings and anxieties with trusted friends;
- Revisit your basic values and set clear priorities based on them;
- Write down your feelings and find someone with whom you can share the writings.

ENFJ Lessons from uncontrolled stress:
- Objectivity and being a bit removed can aid in understanding and acceptance.
- Understand your limitations with a new appreciation.
- It takes many values and perspectives to complete the whole.
- You will survive even when peace and harmony are disrupted.

8 Practical Application

There are volumes written on the practical application of type. We offer here only a few examples from the more popular applications (leadership, communication, learning, and team work). We also offer some references so that you can continue to extend your appreciation of type.

We highly recommend that you look for the application that fits you best. Type applies not only to self-development and the four applications listed above, but also to career planning, coaching, conflict management, consulting, counselling, family, money management, relationships, spiritual development, time management, and most everything in between.

Type is practical. We have said that before. Now, let us introduce you to just a few examples in hopes that you will continue your exploration of both the practical application of type, but also the extension of the theory.

8.1 Leadership

Leadership development and change management is a good place to start. We will give you one short example of how we use type. Type applied to leadership perhaps best fits situational theory. This theory assumes that different situations call for different characteristics, and accordingly there is no single optimal profile of a leader. Leaders must apply different elements of their personality at different times to be most successful. What a person actually does when acting as a leader is, in large part, dependent upon characteristics of the situation. For just one person, this allows for clear acting on preferences, but it also calls for some stretching into less or nonpreferred functions. This can be done, but it is rarely easy. But then, being a leader is not always easy.

Each person has leadership potentials. How a person approaches leadership depends on the type. Invariably, we start with our preferences.

> Bruce stands in front of his team, hands out a copy of the PowerPoint he just presented and makes his point again. He leaves no doubt that the targets are clear for the next two months. Holding up the sheet, pointing his finger again to the definition and the dates listed, he just says "Let's do it – period." As Sandra and Jeff walk out the door, they look at each

other. They don't like his direct style. They don't feel motivated or inspired, just told to do.
Or consider George. He manages a big sales team. He is well liked in the company. He enjoys people, he allows them lots of freedom, and he is authentic. But the catastrophe is approaching – there is no structure, "no effective leadership" the CEO says.

Two opposite types of leaders. Which is best? Which is best for what situation?

The Hersey–Blanchard[9] situational leadership model is one of the more popular theories and when slightly modified it fits type theory very well. Following is an example of the Hersey–Blanchard model with the type applied. If you are familiar with the Hersey–Blanchard model, you will recognize that we have turned the table and provide an ongoing circular model.

Situational Leadership requires movement from one style to another. There is a logic to the movement. That is, in this model the progression generally moves clockwise. Generally, when starting a project or introducing a new product or innovation, we like to have clarity. The ST leader naturally does that quite well. Then, as people understand what they are to do, they often need support and clarification with the tactical approaches. The SF leader provides such specific and concrete tactical support. As time passes, tasks become routine and the motivating inspiration of the NF is most appropriate. Finally, as a project comes to completion, the evaluation and gleaning of what was learned is necessary. This comes most naturally from the NT. This is graphically shown here:

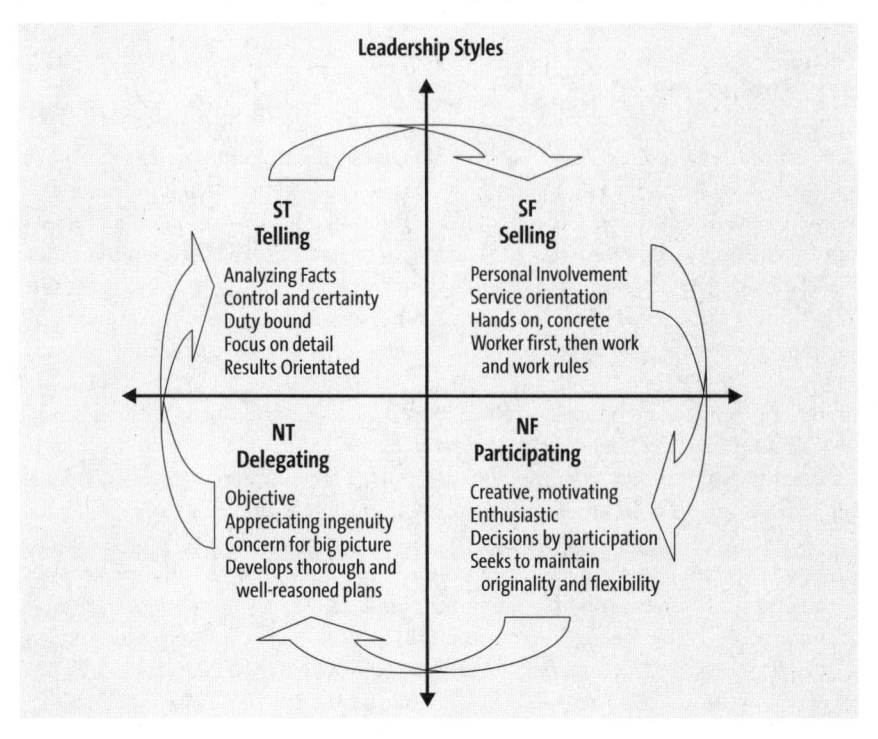

Leadership Styles

ST — Telling
Analyzing Facts
Control and certainty
Duty bound
Focus on detail
Results Orientated

SF — Selling
Personal Involvement
Service orientation
Hands on, concrete
Worker first, then work
and work rules

NT — Delegating
Objective
Appreciating ingenuity
Concern for big picture
Develops thorough and
well-reasoned plans

NF — Participating
Creative, motivating
Enthusiastic
Decisions by participation
Seeks to maintain
originality and flexibility

The most productive approach is to match leadership style with the need of the organization relative to the change desired. For example, let's start with the ST and then progress to the other styles as illustrated in the diagram above.

The ST style is that of telling, directing, or structuring. This style is appropriate when and individual or group is low in ability or willingness and needs direction.

The SF style is that of selling, explaining, persuading, and clarifying. This style is appropriate when the individual or group understands the direction and is working to solidify relationships and align personal goals/missions with the direction set by the organization.

From ST	To SF
Analyzing facts impersonally	Analyzing facts personally
Using a step-by-step process from cause to effect, premise to conclusion	Being concerned about how things matter to selves and others
Emphasizing physical features	Emphasizing interpersonal features
Liking control and certainty	Liking familiarity
Focusing on work rather than worker	Focusing on worker first, then work
Providing specific instructions, and closely supervising performance	Explaining decisions, providing opportunity for clarification
Setting goals to accomplish	Giving support and encouragement
Organizing the work situation	Communicating and involving people
Directing and providing specific instructions	Facilitating people's interactions
Controlling and requiring regular reports	Providing feedback for others
Being the stabilizer/traditionalist – "the powerful take-charge administrator"	Being the trouble shooter/negotiator – "the resourceful problem solver"

The SF style is different from ST in that the leader is not only providing the direction but is also providing the opportunity for dialogue and for clarification. This "selling" enables each person to "buy in" psychologically to what the leader wants. If a leader simply says "I want all employees at their workstations to be working – not eating, reading newspapers, or sleeping," that is telling. On the other hand, if the leader explains, "Eating, reading, and sleeping at workstations is not appropriate – it is against my value system, it is not productive behavior, and it looks bad – now, what are we going to do about it?" that is selling. The follower then can respond with questions of clarification and additional explanation, and must indicate what he/she can "buy into."

Progress continues. At some point the tactics will be completed or become boring. Stimulation, creativity, motivation – something new is needed. As you have been working in the SF style, this ought to have prepared the relational aspects necessary to move into a more participative approach. The SF style will allow setting the necessary alignments and accountabilities while preparing the leader for the next more participative NF style.

From SF	To NF
Analyzing facts personally	Sharing stories about relationships
Being concerned about how things matter to selves and others	Valuing others' concerns and ideas
Emphasizing interpersonal features of the work environment	Highlighting how people are interconnected
Liking familiarity	Cherishing unique contributions
Focusing on worker first, then work	Focusing on growth needs of the people and organization
Explaining decisions and providing opportunity for clarification	Communicating organizational norms and decisions by participation
Giving support	Motivating creatively, encouraging
Facilitating people's interactions	Participating in the process
Providing feedback on people's accomplishments	Sympathizing and commit to the progress of others
Being the trouble shooter/negotiator, the resourceful problem solver	Being the people motivator, persuader, and catalyst

The SF style is that of selling, explaining, persuading, and clarifying. This style is appropriate when the individual or group understands the direction and is working to solidify relationships and align personal goals/missions with the direction set by the organization.

The NF style is that of participating, collaborating, facilitating, or committing. This style is appropriate when the individual or group has just indicated that they are up to the task, but have not had the requisite opportunity to acquire sufficient experience to have confidence in all aspects. High amounts of two-way communication and supportive behavior is necessary, but low levels of guidance. Because they have already shown that they are able to perform the task(s), it isn't necessary to provide substantial direction concerning what to do or how to do it. Discussion and supportive and facilitating behaviors would tend to be more appropriate for solving the problem or soothing the apprehension. Finally, moving from the participating NF to the delegating NT looks something like this:

From NF	To NT
Sharing stories about personal relationships	Ascertaining the worth of the information
Valuing others' concerns and ideas	Ensuring full understanding of the scope and sequence of work
Highlighting how people are interconnected	Analyzing the structure and the process
Cherishing unique contributions	Appreciating ingenuity
Focusing on growth needs of the people and organization	Focusing on mission and systems

From NF	To NT
Valuing people who are cooperative and work in harmony	Valuing competence, intelligence, complexity, and principles
Communicating organizational norms and making decisions by participation	Delegating decision-making and allowing for differing views
Creatively motivating and energizing	Creating vision
Allowing and encouraging people to work together	Building conceptual frameworks, models, and prototypes
Participating in the process	Planning approaches to change or objectively evaluating
Sympathizing and committed to the progress of others	Envisioning how people could do better
Being the people motivator, persuader, and catalyst	Being the firm minded and fair

In summary, the ST style is that of telling, directing, or structuring. This style is appropriate when and individual or group is low in ability or willingness and needs direction.

The SF style is that of selling, explaining, persuading, and clarifying. This style is appropriate when the individual or group understands the direction and is working to solidify relationships and align personal goals/missions with the direction set by the organization.

The NF style is that of participating, collaborating, facilitating, or committing. This style is appropriate when the individual or group has just indicated that they are up to the task, but have not had the requisite opportunity to acquire sufficient experience to have confidence in all aspects.

The NT style is that of delegating, observing, monitoring, and evaluating. This style is appropriate when the individual or group is both ready and willing, or ready and confident. They have had enough opportunity to practice, and they feel comfortable without the leader providing constant direction. At this point it is unnecessary to provide direction about where, what, when, or how because they already understand all of these dimensions and are looking for insight as to how to become better at what they are doing.

Would you like to learn more about type and leadership? We recommend *The Leadership Equation*[11] as a book that addresses how to balance management styles for situational leadership demands and provides a manageable, systematic foundation for building critical people skills. This is a rich source of information on the application of situational leadership. In addition, you may be interested in *Hardwired Leadership*,[12] which provides the tools and step-by-step guidance needed to evaluate strengths, identify blind spots, and plan courses of action for mastering leadership. These resources will extend the number of examples of type and leadership.

8.2 Communication

The preferences we exhibit in how we perceive the world and how we make decisions are demonstrated in how we communicate. If we are moving toward "completion" and "individuation," our communication patterns should reflect that movement. Through periods of differentiation and periods of integration our preferences dictate the tides of communication in a gentle ebb and flow as we always seek to communicate our connectedness with those around us. Psychological type theory provides an avenue by which we can come to better understand these communication differences and put them to practical use.

Whenever people differ, the possibilities for misunderstandings increase. Moreover, communication, at times, seems to point to the chasm between the differences. Yet, we can attain communication skills that empower us to exchange ideas and resources powerfully and accurately.

To serve a useful purpose, communication needs to be listened to, understood, and considered without hostility in a spirit of resolution and reconciliation. It is human nature to ignore messages if we have the impression that what is being said is going to be irrelevant or unimportant. We condition each other quite quickly to expect either important information or unimportant information.

Any communication needs to establish immediately that it promises something of worth. The trouble is that what is considered worthwhile varies from type to type. This is especially true in the differences between extraverted types, who are energized by others, and the introverted types, who are energized by ideas and introspection. The extravert is likely to say something of worth at some point – because they try to communicate everything. They need to be mindful to get quickly to the important aspects of the message. The introvert, on the other hand, may hesitate too long in any interaction. Consider trying to share a lengthy, exciting story with someone like Austrian author and poet Rainer Maria Rilke, who once stated, "the necessity to be alone, alone for a long time, builds in me everyday... People (whether it be my fault or theirs) wear me out." If we do not appreciate the sources of energy of different people we are not likely to grasp the true meaning of the messages they send.

We also have found that communications frequently carry concurrent messages both about what is perceived and about judgments of the perceptions. While this makes communication lively and interesting, it also creates problems. For example:

> *A mother and her 15-year-old daughter came in for counseling. In the course of the conversation the counselor asked the mother to identify one thing her daughter was doing that she would like to change. The mother said, "She is totally irresponsible." The daughter was quick to react to the statement, saying, "That is not so." The counselor pointed out to the mother that she was asked to identify what the daughter did, not what she thought the daughter was for doing it. The mother then said, "She thinks she is the only one in the family." Again the daughter responded, "That is*

not so." Again the counselor pointed out to the mother that she was giving an evaluation or judgment, not an identification of what her daughter did. The mother thought for a minute and then said, *"That is hard to do. Everything that comes to mind is an evaluation."*

This is not surprising, especially if the mother's dominant function is thinking or feeling (one of the judgment functions).

Learning to differentiate among the functions is not always easy. We must strive to clearly express our perceptions – both sensing and intuition. And we ought to be sensitive and fair when we communicate our judgments – both thinking and feeling. We easily mix up what we observe with how we evaluate or place worth. Our language is an important instrument that invites us to talk about stability and constants – about similarities. Yet we try to symbolize with this language a world of process, change, differences, interactions, and complexity. Indeed, we face a challenge whenever we attempt to communicate.

We can learn, however, to interact in more interesting ways. No person has to be good at everything. But, if you are able to use your own strengths and preferences, and in turn appreciate the other person's strengths and preferences, it is possible to truly make use of a wider range of human resources. Together, thanks to our differences, we can all extend our abilities. We realize the importance of recognizing that individual differences affect interpersonal communication and thus affect the tasks and relationships at hand.

Assuming that we first can distinguish and can learn to differentiate those communications intended to share perceptions from those that articulate judgments, we recognize that there will be specific preferences for how perceptions are shared. A person with a preference for sensing places high faith in what is actual and factual, and will communicate clear and precise information. When presented with an idea, the sensor's natural reaction is to concentrate on the specifics and, frequently, to identify what is missing. Sensors will identify particular realistic ramifications as to why an idea may not work. They are literal, and will be looking for the concrete data in any communication. They might find it helpful if you use phrases such as "it might work if..." and "have you considered using..." before bringing up the objections that experience suggests. You should anticipate the specific questions that the sensor is sure to ask. For example, sensors will tend to ask questions such as; "What would you do about Mr. Schmidt? He weighs 300 pounds, and we have only 15-inch metal folding chairs?" Then they will listen carefully for your response.

When communicating with a sensor, it is wise to clarify and articulate the details. Define your terms, be clear about facts, and have a definite plan of action so that the sensor can get right to work. You will receive specific answers to any specific questions. We are communicating perceptions and receiving information; no judgments or evaluations are made.

The person with a preference for intuition is, by nature, an idea person. When an intuitor comes up with a blazing new insight, the natural course is often to present it in a rough and sketchy form. When listening to an intuitive type, concentrate on the main point (if you can identify it) and ignore the incomplete details. Again, we are talking about perception here, no judgments please.

When presenting an idea to an intuitive type, know your main point. Remember, they are not literal like the sensor – they are relational. Do not list a million details and facts; intuitors are not interested in all of these details, unless, of course, you want to try to link them. If you need help with an idea, ask "Generally speaking, what would you consider doing in this instance?" The intuitor will happily expend time and energy to help you think through the myriad of possible obstacles.

Just as perceptions are communicated in radically different terms, so, too, judgments are expressed in quite distinct manners. Thinkers decide logically and may forget to reckon with the seemingly illogical human motives and reactions that are part of any interpersonal situation. They, therefore, tend to state their positions bluntly, without particular concern for the feelings of the other people involved. A thinker needs to be reminded, calmly and matter-of-factly, how other people feel. They then can count people's feelings among the causes to be factored into the decision, and identify appropriate actions accordingly.

Feeling types, on the other hand, set great value upon harmony and good will in their decisions, and are very aware of the likes and dislikes of people around them. They may assume that others are equally aware of feelings. This is often a faulty assumption and a feeler may find calm assertive communication skills useful when presenting the feeling aspects of the situation.

A thinker talking with feelers should remember that feelers prize harmony and would prefer to agree, if given a chance. Therefore, with feelers we might begin the discussion by mentioning the points of agreement. After this tone is set, points of difference can be carefully presented, discussed, negotiated, and finally celebrated.

A feeler talking with thinkers should remember that thinkers value logic and rationality. Thinkers do not have to always agree. They can differ greatly if rules of logic are honored. A feeler may initiate a discussion by outlining a logical progression, and then allowing the thinkers to debate the issues without coming to consensus.

When communicating perceptions, consider:
- Sensing types take facts more seriously than possibilities; they want an explicit statement of the problem before considering possible solutions.
- Intuitive types want the prospect of an interesting possibility before they buckle down to the facts.

When communicating judgments, consider:
- Thinkers demand that a statement have a beginning, a logically arranged sequence of points, and an end. They especially need an identifiable objective, and are impatient with repetition and rambling detail.
- Feeling types are interested mainly in matters that have a definite effect on people; if you start with a concern for people, they listen.

When compromise between opposite types is necessary, the best position is one that considers what each type holds as important. The sensing type wants the solution to be workable; the intuitive wants the door left open for growth and improvement. Thinkers want the solution to be systematic; feelers want the solution to be humanly agreeable.

A good idea can be presented from any one of these angles if we are sensitive in our communication. All types will feel justified in attacking something that seems wrong to them. The trouble here is that any attack is likely to provoke a posture of defense and a breakdown of communication between individuals, instead of a united celebration of differences and enriched communication patterns.

When presenting, influencing, or trying to understand:

S-Types	N-Types
Are factual	Give global scheme
Document successful applications	Seize opportunity
Reduce risk factors	Use confidence and enthusiasm
Work out details in advance	Indicate challenges
Show why it makes sense	Point out the future benefits
T-Types	**F-Types**
Are objective	Explain who else likes the idea
State principles involved	Are personable and friendly
Stress competence	Indicate how it helps others
List costs and benefits	Tell why it is valuable
Are calm and reasonable	Are personable and friendly

Consider your preferred communication style. Do you resonate with the descriptions above? Can you identify other people with different preferences? Explore the ways in which you can communicate better with other preferred styles.

Would you like to learn more about type and communication? *The Communication Wheel*[13] is a practical system for using psychological type to improve communication. The wheel itself is an easily understood model that visually represents all 16 types and their relationship to each other, making it easy to see why communication problems exist and what to do about them. Counselors, educators, families, and business leaders benefit from this simple, direct approach with applications for problem solving, leader development, team building, conflict resolution, quality management, change management, customer service, and diversity issues.

In addition, with today's emphasis on team-based and collaborative management and decision making, communication can make or break an organization you may find *Introduction to Type and Communication*[14] helpful. This booklet provides a concise overview of communication skills and strategies, practical tips for communicating with others, and developmental tips for each of the 16 types, as well as an introduction to differences in communication styles.

8.3 Learning

The way in which we prefer to learn is grounded in type. All learners – young and old – have decided preferences for learning. Some like the quiet library for reading, reflection, and pondering thoughts. Others learn best through lively debate and animated discussion. Educators take these differences into account as they approach their students. Parents can also enhance the parent–child relationship through the use of type. We all have much to learn from each other.

> *Daughter Erin was having problems because she was required to start her thesis by creating an outline. As she struggled, frustrations grew. Finally, we suggested that she just write out her thoughts – a free-flow of ideas. She loved doing that. Then when she finished, we went back through and teased out the outline. Done.*

Erin prefers NF and did not want to be bound by tightly structured outlines and organized rules, especially when she was telling her story. Allow each person to tell their story in a way that comes most natural for them.

> *We were working in the dining room as we saw the bicycle speeding down the street. We realized it was Marcel as he turned into the driveway. He jumped off the bike (still at full speed) and the bike crashed into the bushes about the same time Marcel burst in the front door. He ran up the stairs, two at a time, and stood in front of the computer and music keyboard. Seconds later, he came bounding down the stairs, glanced at us in the dining room and said "Got it" as he disappeared out the door, retrieved his bike from the bushes and headed off down the street.*

We just smiled at each other. We knew that NF Marcel needed to grab that great melodic passage before it was lost. We were pleased that Marcel exercised the "discipline" to capture what was on his mind. He had learned how best to take advantage of his learning preferences – and not lose his briallantly great spur-of-the-moment ideas.

> *As liberal and enlightened parents, we would invariably respond to Rachel with questions. When she would do something wrong, we would query; "What do you think your punishment should be?" Or when she would want to go out and play, we would say; "What is a good time for someone your age to return home?" This was a rather typical pattern for us as parents – we wanted Rachel to grow up to be independent, making her own decisions and taking full control of her life. Then when she was 12 years old, we introduced her to personality type. The instant she learned that her parents were strong intuitives (NT and NF) and she preferred SF, she declared: "Now I know why you do not give me exact answers – you can't."*

Well, of course we could have given her the precision she needed, but we didn't – at least not very often. It was a good lesson for us parents to learn that we have the responsibility to provide structure in general, and to initiate concrete, exact responses out of respect for our SF daughter.

Professors, teachers, and parents, as educators, ought to appreciate the individual uniqueness of each learner.[14] The following basic patterns of teaching and learning are gleaned from type theory:

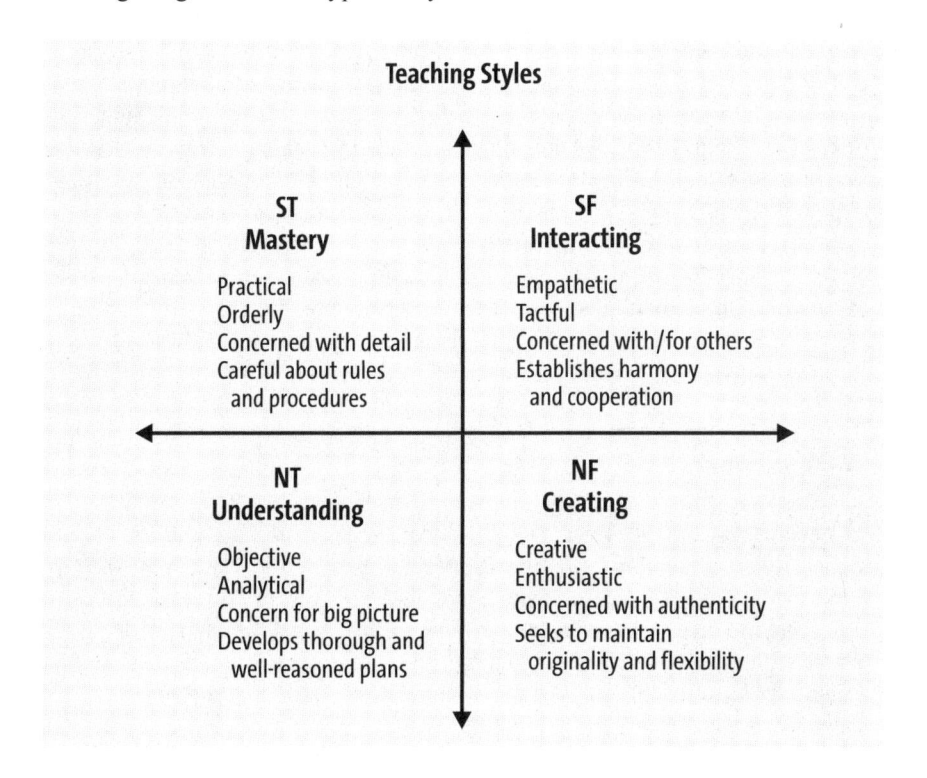

Teaching Styles

ST Mastery	SF Interacting
Practical Orderly Concerned with detail Careful about rules and procedures	Empathetic Tactful Concerned with/for others Establishes harmony and cooperation
NT **Understanding**	**NF** **Creating**
Objective Analytical Concern for big picture Develops thorough and well-reasoned plans	Creative Enthusiastic Concerned with authenticity Seeks to maintain originality and flexibility

Giving students options is an effective way to enhance the learning experience. We recommend that each lesson be designed in at least four ways to accommodate the function pairs.

We also need to appreciate what others offer and learn from what they offer.

We all knew that Denise was dying. She had struggled with cancer for some time, and now the end was near. Natalia was with Denise those last days when we received a tear-soaked email. "Denise sadly passed away. My heart is heavy, we will all miss her. Grieving touches all that I can feel. I know that she is at peace, and that is some comfort. Love, Natalia."

Yes, we understood the message. We also understood Natalia. Preferences for NF, the caring, comforting, and feeling all came through. No details, however.

The only fact was that Denise had passed on. We had to wait to get the details of time, place, and the like from others. We did not expect anything other than feelings at this point from Natalia. We had learned long ago that she would provide the concern for others, and now again she reminded us of that.

The following resources are helpful for teachers and parents alike: *Looking at Type and Learning Styles*[16] is written for both students and teachers. This book helps gain insight into personal learning styles to develop more effective study and test-taking strategies and help teachers facilitate learning. Strengths, key motivators, and blind spots for different preferences are offered and guidelines are provided to assist teachers in curriculum development and delivery.

We also recommend *Effective Teaching, Effective Learning*,[17] which was written to help teachers bridge the gap between their teaching techniques and the needs of their students. The authors show teachers how to identify the strengths and potential limitations of their own natural teaching styles and explain why certain styles are more effective with some students than others. Easy-to-use methods provide the means for reaching students whose preferred learning style may be different from the instructor's favored teaching method. It is filled with concrete examples, practical techniques, and diagnostic aids.

8.4 Teamwork

Concrete performance results – that's what teams are all about. When the goals of a team do not define specific results that are important to overall company goals, the accomplishments will rarely be very powerful. After all, performance challenges are what create real teams to begin with. If a strong performance ethic is lacking or if a company's over goals are unclear of confused, teams either will not form or, if they do, will fall significantly short of their potential.[17].

Productively functioning teams all report a clear understanding that team members sink or swim together, are linked by common bonds, and meet frequently both formally and informally – yet they are made up of individuals that may be quite different one from another. Fully functioning teams exercise collaborative skills reflecting often on how well they are doing and experience a common bonding to ensure differences are taken in account. The empirical evidence is overwhelming: When a small group of people challenge themselves to climb over a wall or up a mountain or through a desert – or to reduce cycle time by 50% – their respective titles, perks, and other "stripes" fade into the background.

An effective group or team is based on a set of interpersonal relationships structured to achieve established goals and to create new goals for themselves. Teams function as individual members interact. The productivity of teams is not a simple additive function of team members' technical competencies and

8 Practical Application 129

task abilities. Productivity is not guaranteed just because all team members have an interest in attaining the teams' goals. Successful team performance requires interpersonal competencies and a processing of those competencies that ensures the group of motivated individuals will work together productively.

Type gives a language to talk about the differences as well as pointing to the strengths different individuals bring to the team.

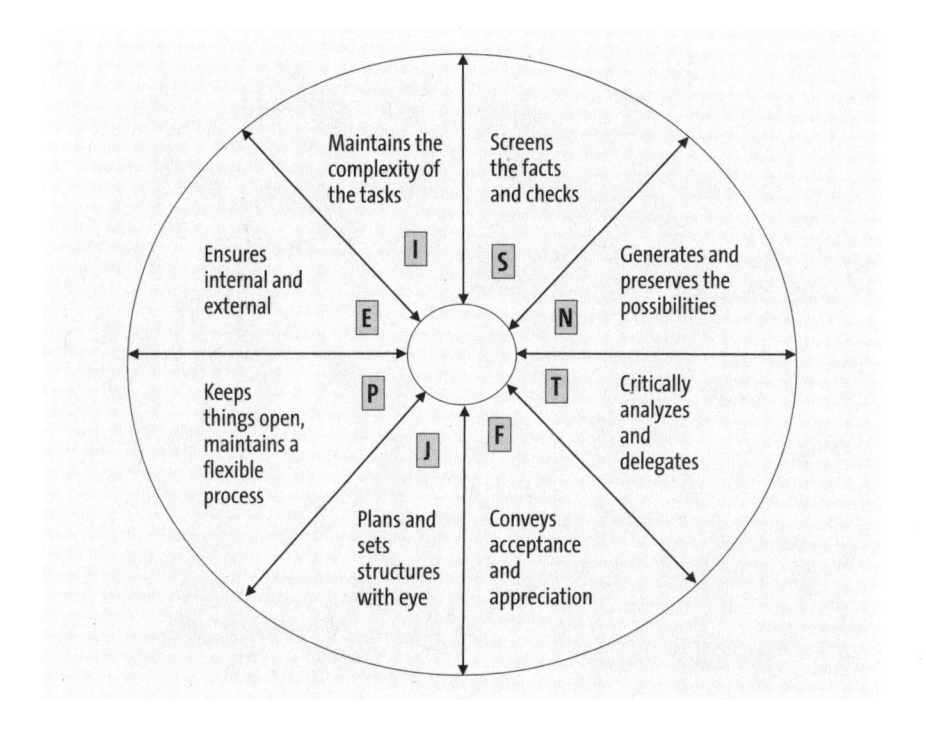

As you look around the circle, you will note that all of these attributes are necessary for team success. The challenge is to bring all of the uniqueness to focus on the task at hand.

Turning Team Performance Inside Out[19] is a resource that may just help. In this unique approach to improving team performance, Susan Nash utilizes type theory to analyze teams from the inside out. She demonstrates how individuals can discover patterns of behavior, create and interpret a team profile, and design customized performance improvement strategies with immediate results. Using case studies, self-assessments, exercises, and real-life profiles of teams in action, Nash demonstrates how to anticipate and overcome challenges, diagnose potential problems, and capitalize on individual and team strengths.

Remember the saying "two heads are better than one?" Well, a team brings together a diversity of talent and experience and can have better flexibility than individuals working on their own. But the trick is to get those individual members to perform in concert to make a strong and effective team. *Leading Teams*[20] explains how a leader's ability to create strategies and offer support can help team members manage themselves. We trust that you will find this yet another practical application of type.

9 Summary

We could go on, but each book must end somewhere. This is where we choose to leave you – with practical application on your mind.

Share with us your stories. What have you learned? What are your questions? How can we help you in your endeavors? Our stories build. Theories are enhanced and applications expand. Our learning continues and our quest for completion is unending.

10 References

1. Jung, C. G. (1976). *Collected works of C. G. Jung, Volume 6: Psychological types* (G. Adler & R. F. C. Hull, Trans., Eds.). Princeton, NJ: Princeton University Press.
2. Kretschmer, E. (1967). *Körperbau und Charakter* [Physique and Character] (25th ed.). Berlin: Springer. (Original work published 1921).
3. Myers, I. B., McCaulley, M. H., Quenk, N. L., & Hammer, A. L. (1998). *MBTI manual: A guide to the development and use of the Myers-Briggs type indicator* (3rd ed.). Palo Alto, CA: Consulting Psychologists Press.
4. Golden, J. (2004). *Golden personality type profiler*. Austin, TX: Psychological Corporation.
5. Wheelright, J., Wheelright, J., & Buehler, J. (1978). *Jungian type survey: The Gray-Wheelwright test manual* (16th revision). San Francisco: Society of Jungian Analysts of Northern California.
6. Singer, J., & Loomis, M. (1996). *Interpretive guide for the Singer-Loomis Type Deployment Inventory*. Gresham, OR: Moving Boundaries.
7. Ødegård, T., & Ringstad, H. E. (2001). *Understanding Jungian type: A practical guide*. Bergen, Norway: Optimas Organisasjonspsykologene AS.
8. Huether, G. (1996). The Central Adaption Syndrome: Psychological stress as a trigger for adaptive modifications of brain structure and brain function. *Progress in Neurobiology, 48*, 569–612.
9. Quenk, N. (1993). *Beside ourselves: Our hidden personality in everyday life*. Palo Alto, CA: Davies-Black.
10. Hersey, P., Blanchard, K., & Johnons, D. (2007). *Management of organizational behavior* (9th ed.). Upper Saddle River, NJ: Prentice-Hall.
11. Barr, L., & Barr, N. (1989). *The leadership equation*. Austin, TX: Eakin Press.
12. Pearman, R. (1998). *Hard wired leadership*. Yarmouth, ME: Intercultural Press.
13. Thompson, H. (2000). *The communication wheel*. Watkinsville, GA: Wormhole Publishing.
14. Dunning, D. (2003). *Introduction to type and communication*. Palo Alto, CA: CPP.
15 Bents, R., & Howey, K. (1981). Staff development – Change in the individual. In *1981 ASCC yearbook staff development/organizational development*. Alexandria, VA: Association for Supervision and Curriculum Development.
16. Lawrence, G. (1997). *Looking at type and learning styles*. Gainesville, FL: Center for Applications of Psychological Type.
17. Fairshurst, A. M., & Farihurst, L. (2002). *Effective teaching, effective learning*. Gainesville, FL: Center for Applications of Psychological Type.
18. Katzenbach, J. R., & Smith, D. K. (2003). *The wisdom of teams: Creating the high-performance organization*. New York, NY: Harper Business.
19. Nash, S. (1999). *Turning team performance inside out*. Mountain View, CA: Davies-Black.
20. Hackman, M. R. (2002). *Leading teams: Setting the stage for great performances*. Boston, MA: Harvard Business School Press.